W9-CFO-123

DEMOCRATIC ETHICAL EDUCATIONAL LEADERSHIP

Democratic Ethical Educational Leadership presents a cohesive framework for aspiring and practicing leaders to explore the complex nature of leadership while supporting democratic citizenry and social responsibility in turbulent times. Organized around the five "New DEEL" visions for leadership, the chapters illustrate real people who embody these principles. This critical resource provides pathways for aspiring ethical leaders to integrate democracy, social justice, and school reform through dialogue and deliberation. Combining diverse and vibrant exemplars in action with a compelling vision for leadership, this book will inspire educational leaders to reflect upon their practice and reach their potential as democratic ethical leaders.

Special features include:

- a unique framework to guide responsible, ethical leadership in today's schools;
- case studies to help readers identify key leadership qualities in context from which to illuminate their own emerging practice;
- for instructors, helpful ideas to use the case studies in authentic classroom settings;
- end-of-chapter questions to encourage exploration of leaders' motivations, processes, strategies, and lessons learned.

Steven Jay Gross is Professor of Educational Leadership at the College of Education, Temple University, USA, and Founding Director of the New DEEL Community Network.

Joan Poliner Shapiro is Professor of Higher Education at the College of Education, Temple University, USA, and Co-Director of the New DEEL Community Network.

DEMOCRATIC ETHICAL EDUCATIONAL LEADERSHIP

RECLAIMING SCHOOL REFORM

Steven Jay Gross and Joan Poliner Shapiro

Routledge
Taylor & Francis Group

NEW YORK AND LONDON

First published 2016
by Routledge, 711 Third Avenue, New York, NY 10017

and by Routledge
2 Park Square, Milton Park, Abingdon, Oxon, OX14 4RN

Routledge is an imprint of the Taylor & Francis Group, an informa business

Library of Congress Cataloging-in-Publication Data
Gross, Steven Jay.
   Democratic ethical educational leadership : reclaiming school
reform / by Steven Jay Gross & Joan Poliner Shapiro.
      pages cm
   1. School improvement programs—United States.   2. Educational
leadership—Moral and ethical aspects—United States.   I. Shapiro,
Joan Poliner.   II. Title.
   LB2822.82.G76 2015
   371.2'07—dc23   2015008610

ISBN: 978-0-415-83954-9 (hbk)
ISBN: 978-0-415-83955-6 (pbk)
ISBN: 978-0-203-77112-9 (ebk)

Typeset in New Baskerville
by Apex CoVantage, LLC

Printed and bound in the United States of America by Publishers Graphics,
LLC on sustainably sourced paper.

From Steve: For Will, Emily, and Justin. You take the values of democratic ethical living everywhere you go. I am so proud of you.

From Joan: For Dr. Suzie Shapiro, the embodiment of a New DEEL educational leader and a caring daughter and mother, and for Mark Edlitz, a writer about superheroes as exemplars and a compassionate son-in-law and father.

From us both: We want to dedicate our book to the scholars and practitioners all around the world who have taken the New DEEL vision for educational leadership to heart and are making it a reality for their students. You are true exemplars!

Contents

Foreword

This book is an excellent example of the ongoing work of a loosely allied group of international scholars committed to the promotion and study of ethical school leadership. Virtually all of the authors are members or associates of a University Council for Educational Administration (UCEA) program center, established in 1996, called the Consortium for the Study of Leadership and Ethics in Education (CSLEE). For almost twenty years now, this group of scholars has devoted itself to the study of values and ethics in school leadership. Their ranks include many world-class scholars.

The two authors of this book, Gross and Shapiro, are certainly to be recognized as primary players in the work of the CSLEE and significant contributors to the development of the theory and practice of ethical school leadership. What was during the mid-1990s a rather scattered, narrow, and polarized body of theory and research has now evolved to a more coherent field of inquiry—international in scope, sharing a common vocabulary of terms, and increasingly relevant to practitioners working in the context of educational leadership. This book reflects well that consolidation of theory and conceptual models. But it goes further than that by modeling and adopting as its organizing structure a particular and very effective approach to promoting dialogue and learning on ethical school leadership. The key dimensions of this approach are the utilization of real-life case studies of educational practice and a multi-ethical analysis and interpretation process.

The use of case studies as a basis for leadership development is not a new approach. It has been a primary instructional strategy of school leadership development programs for decades, particularly in Canada and the United States. However, the approach reflected in this book demonstrates the sophistication that comes from years of experience and a thoughtful pedagogy that is the outcome of a commitment to deep transformational learning and social responsibility. The case studies presented in these chapters are real-life experiences, not hypothetical. More importantly, the cases do not promote a single set of right answers. Rather, they demonstrate and promote a habit of reflective practice that recognizes that, as important as ethics are, they must always be considered in a context. The cases also demonstrate how ethics can be notoriously vulnerable to misuse as either justifications for self-serving actions by individuals, or being applied by the power brokers of a society as absolute values intended to protect their own interests at the expense of the poor, the disadvantaged, or the voiceless.

This leads to a final point. There is an element of outrage and determined purpose reflected in this book. Despite the fact that ethical school leadership as a concept has become almost mainstream in recent years, and the huge progress scholars have achieved in terms of consolidating theory, conceptual frameworks, and models over the past twenty years, we still encounter the superficial application of ethics as absolute values, cynically adopted to perpetuate existing social orders that are anything but just. And, even in the admittedly less high-stakes context of scholarly writing, we still encounter those who think that simply citing an ethic in an opening paragraph about someone makes them thoughtful reflective practitioners. The writers of the chapters in this book show us a better way to becoming genuinely democratic ethical leaders. However, they also caution us that, although this may be the right way and the better way, it is not necessarily the easier way.

Paul T. Begley
Executive Director
UCEA Consortium for the Study of Leadership and
Ethics in Education

Chapter 1

Introduction

We write this book in a time of danger, fear, vast hope, and opportunity. If you are reminded of Dickens's famed opening lines from *A Tale of Two Cities* ("It was the best of times, it was the worst of times . . ."), that is understandable. Perhaps it is the fate of all generations to hold such reflections. Yet, standing in what is still the threshold of a new millennium, wondrous advancement seems more thoroughly juxtaposed with the advent of hideous disaster than ever. If it is the inevitable human reflection to hold these extremes out as the salient descriptors of one's times, we have no less a claim than previous generations. For the first time in history, we have the possibility of housing, feeding, and caring for all of humanity, yet we live in a world of vast inequity and want. Our technology creates mass communication unthinkable a generation ago, but this creativity is often perverted to the cause of hideous animosities, leading to brutality we too soon thought relegated to a dark past. Tumultuous conditions in security, economics, the environment, and our exposure to technology-driven change abound. In light of these turbulent forces, is it any wonder that our ties are characterized by insecurity and fear for our children's future?

At such times our education policy apparatus responds in a consistent, albeit worrisome, manner. For generations it has been our habit to focus on schools as the reason for our peril as well as the locus of our salvation. In 1957 the Soviet Union launched *Sputnik*, the first orbiting satellite, thereby beating the U.S. in technology and igniting the space race. We may have questioned our scientific community, but the real outrage for this perceived failure (the U.S. did soon catch up to the Soviets) was directed at America's schools—specifically a supposed spirit of complacency that threatened our security. In 1983, the same arguments were employed in the Nation at Risk report, the Reagan administration's attack on public schools and the now infamous "rising tide of mediocrity" that they represented. While this trend is as unfounded as it is illogical, demands for urgent changes in P-20 education have become a national reflex. In our globalized economy, this reflex transcends borders and is now standard fare among policy makers in nearly every advanced economy.

Yet powerful concepts such as education reform are neither simple nor monolithic in their meaning. Attention must be paid to the details of projects traveling under such banners. In a recent article, one of us (Gross, 2014a) pointed to the positive image that reformers have in many cultures. In that same article, the complexity of reform itself was analyzed. Over the past century, progressives, essentialists, perennialists, and existentialists have all initiated their own brand of educational reform. In our time, in the wake of what Berliner and Biddle (1995) call the "manufactured crisis," education reform seems to be confined to a marriage of two allied traditions: essentialism and market forces. The former is in the guise of high-stakes tests, top-down standards, and harsh sanctions; and the latter emphasizes privatization, the end of teacher unions, and charter schools that are frequently owned by private corporations with fiduciary responsibilities to stockholders rather than communities. With a constant drum beat decrying the supposed mediocrity of public schools and their implied complicity in causing and sustaining the achievement gap, it is little wonder that the brand of reform has nearly monopolized public discourse.

Critics of this policy direction object to the notion that one size fits all (Ohanian, 1999), which they claim is currently the case with standards linked to high-stakes tests and the resulting narrowed curriculum (Ravitch, 2010). Many of the same dissenting educators and a growing number of the public question the premise that changes in schools alone can create a fairer society, or that refashioning schools into the factory-like settings they once were—where students become both raw material and unpaid workers—is a fitting way to respond to the democratic premise of public education. Focusing on the market forces facet of the current reform policies, researchers question the claims that charter schools yield better results than their public school counterparts—the picture being far too nuanced for such sweeping claims (Miron, Urschel, Mathis, & Tornquist, 2010; Ravitch, 2013).

Looking at the landscape of this brand of education reform from a higher altitude, one finds even more disturbing problems. Whereas knowledge is ever expanding, educators and the students in their charge find themselves pitted against one another as they compete for ever-higher test results. Education itself seems twisted from its original mission of expanding our experience in the world into a dreary pursuit of manufacturing quietly efficient workers at all levels. Recent critiques of this phenomenon at our most prestigious universities, such as Deresiewicz's *Excellent Sheep* (2014), illustrate this point.

The market forces brand of school reform raises high the banner of treating students and their families as customers. Critics believe this stretches the business metaphor to the point that it obscures one salient reality: the move from citizen to customer is a descent into transactional relationships, devoid of rights and community connections. For instance, one has a right to attend public school, but one typically must apply to attend a charter school. People only have access to businesses to the extent that they have resources to purchase services from those entities. By contrast, citizens have rights to share the public sphere, be it at the park, the library, or the local public school. The reverse is true. We have responsibilities to public enterprises that transcend our personal use. Our taxes go to support the park, the library, and the school, whether or not we use them.

Looked at another way, public enterprises compel us to define "we" in a larger, more inclusive way. But customers owe very little to the businesses they frequent. In fact, the competitive marketplace sits upon the premise that customers make decisions based on self-interest, taking their custom where they will. There is such a thing as brand loyalty, of course, but it hardly seems sturdy enough a bond to hold a society together. In a postagrarian world, we all must be consumers to some degree. But the phrase "consumer society" falls far short of the mark when it comes to the qualities needed to sustain even a semblance of a democratic ethical culture for us and for our children.

Education reform is certainly needed, but it is a qualitatively different kind of reform, based on a distinct vision for leadership and categorically different values than the ones described above.[1] *The purpose of this book is to help reclaim school reform by advocating democratic ethical leadership in education.* We do not accept the notion that students and their families need to be passive consumers locked into a dreary contest for their future. We believe that our schools, from early childhood to graduate school, need to inspire truly democratic ethical participatory cultures. We do not say this lightly, nor have we come to this conclusion recently.

BACKGROUND OF THE NEW DEEL

Even as neoliberals argued that rising test scores and market forces could diminish income inequalities and high rates of poverty, another narrative was emerging. Scholars in the field of educational administration called for more progressive, ethical, and democratic forms of renewal for schools in

4 STEVEN JAY GROSS AND JOAN POLINER SHAPIRO

the U.S. and abroad (Aiken, 2002; Begley, 1999; Begley & Zaretsky, 2004; Boyd, 2000; Davis, 2003; Gross, 2004b; Reitzug & O'Hair, 2002; Sernak, 1998; Shapiro & Purpel, 2004; Shapiro & Stefkovich, 2011; Starratt, 2004; Young, Petersen, & Short, 2002).

These writers were part of a long tradition linking social justice and democracy with education. Jane Addams and Ellen Gates Starr made the same connection at Hull House (Addams, 2002), as did Hilda Worthington Smith at the Bryn Mawr Summer School for Women Workers in Industry (Smith, 1929). At the height of the Great Depression, Franklin D. Roosevelt initiated the Civilian Conservation Corps for unemployed men, also based on much the same logic, while Eleanor Roosevelt made a valiant effort to offer the same kind of program for women (Cook, 1999; Gross, 2004a).

Those educational administration scholars questioning neoliberalism in the 21st century also drew inspiration from the democratic administration movement of the 1930s and 1940s in the U.S. The parallel between the two eras seemed apt; the U.S. faced harsh economic times in the Depression. At the turn of this century, the technology bubble had burst and our economic future seemed dimmed. The U.S. faced a threat to its democracy from Fascist Italy, Nazi Germany, and Imperial Japan, and now faces an era of terror, war, and challenges to civil liberties in the post-9/11 world. Therefore, it is instructive to recall our field's reaction in school leadership programs in the 1930s and 1940s, which was to emphasize democratic power-sharing among administrators, teachers, and parents. The works of Harold Rugg and Alice Miel of Teachers College (Kliebard, 1987; Koopman, Miel, & Misner, 1943); George Counts (1932); and the career of Ella Flagg Young in developing teacher councils when she served as the first woman school superintendent of a major U.S. city (Webb & McCarthy, 1998) all undergirded this movement.

Central to the thinking of this group of 21st-century scholars was the philosophy of Ella Flagg Young's colleague John Dewey. In *The School and Society* (1900), Dewey railed against education that sought to mold children like so much raw material:

I may have exaggerated somewhat in order to make plain the typical points of the old education: its passivity of attitude, its mechanical massing of children, its uniformity of curriculum and method. It may be summed up by stating that the center of gravity is outside the child. It is in the teacher, the textbook, anywhere and everywhere you please except in the immediate instincts and activities of the child himself.

(Dewey, 1900, p. 34)

But leaders of the emerging movement also looked at contemporary international leaders for inspiration. In *God Has a Dream*, Archbishop

Desmond Tutu's (2005) description of *ubuntu* illustrates the potential of democratic ethical educational leadership:

> According to ubuntu, it is not a great good to be successful through being aggressively competitive and succeeding at the expense of others. In the end, our purpose is social and communal harmony and well-being. Ubuntu does not say, "I think, therefore I am." It says rather, "I am human because I belong. I participate. I share." Harmony, friendliness, community are great goods. Social harmony is for us the *summum bonum—the* greatest good. Anything that subverts, that undermines this sought-after good is to be avoided like the plague. Anger, resentment, lust for revenge, even success through aggressive competitiveness, are corrosive of this good.
>
> (p. 27)

In 2004, we decided to take action and moved to organize other like-minded educational administration academics and field administrators. We agreed on the name "New DEEL," standing for Democratic Ethical Educational Leadership, and challenged ourselves with the daunting job of changing the direction of educational administration in the U.S. and abroad.

EARLY DEVELOPMENT

Almost immediately, we shared our vision for a new movement in educational administration with faculty and department leaders from the Pennsylvania State University, the University of Vermont, Rowan University, the University of Oklahoma, the University Council of Educational Administration, and the University of North Carolina at Greensboro, as well as U.S. and Canadian practitioner leaders. The group agreed that democratic citizenship and ethical leadership were the top priorities for our educational system in any era, and especially in the new century, where violence, economic dislocation, and environmental degradation were daily news events. To develop the New DEEL, two winter strategy sessions were held at Temple University, the first in 2005 and the second in 2006. These sessions resulted in refining the concept of the New DEEL, its implications for educational administration programs, and a mission statement that united the group. The New DEEL's mission statement focuses on these values:

> The mission of the New DEEL is to create an action-oriented partnership, dedicated to inquiry into the nature and practice of democratic, ethical educational leadership through sustained processes of open dialogue, right to voice, com- munity inclusion, and responsible participation toward the common good. We strive to create an environment to facilitate democratic ethical

decision-making in educational theory and practice which acts in the best interest of all students.

(Gross & Shapiro, 2005, p. 1)

Gross (2009) described the emerging values of the group in this way:

New DEEL members believe that the first job of the school is to help young people become effective citizens in a democracy. Learning how to earn a living is crucial, but it is a close second, in their opinion. Democratic citizenship in any era is a complex task, but it seems especially difficult in our era where international conflict and growing economic and social inequality are the rule. New DEEL members consider the either/or choice among school improvement, democracy and social justice . . . to be a false dilemma. They believe, instead, that there is no democracy without social justice, no social justice without democracy, and that these mutually inclusive concepts are indispensable ingredients to school improvement worthy of the name.

(p. 262)

The group's concept of educational leadership applies to teachers, students, parents, and community members just as much as to the person sitting at the principal's desk. Moreover, to respond to the challenges of our era, educational leaders needed to move beyond their buildings, and their school system's structure, to make alliances with community leaders in areas such as health care and commerce.

The New DEEL group quickly grew from a handful of academics, mostly in the U.S., to include educational administration faculty from over 30 universities and practitioner colleagues in Canada, Australia, Taiwan, Sweden, the UK, Hong Kong, New Zealand, and Jamaica, as well as the U.S. The group dedicated itself to scholarship, curriculum development, and community-building through conferences. Significant progress in all three areas has been made over the past decade.[2]

All of this was inspiring, but soon people asked just what a New DEEL leader was going to look like, and what difference there was between this person and the typical educational administrator. The mission statement set a general direction aimed at reclaiming a more progressive, socially just, and responsive school system, but now specifics were required. In response, the New DEEL vision for educational leadership was developed (Gross, 2009).

THE FIVE QUALITIES OF NEW DEEL

Table 1.1 contrasts the five qualities of the New DEEL vision for educational leadership with the corresponding qualities of more conventional leaders.

Table 1.1 New DEEL Vision for Leaders (Gross, 2009)

New DEEL Vision for Educational Leaders	*Behavior of Conventional School Leaders*
1. **Guided by inner sense of Responsibility to students, faculty, staff, families, the community and social development on a world scale.**	Driven by an exterior pressure of accountability to those above in the organizational/political hierarchy.
2. **Leads from an expansive community- building perspective. A democratic actor who understands when and how to *shield* the school from turbulence and when and how to *use* turbulence to facilitate change.**	Bound by the system and the physical building. A small part of a monolithic, more corporate structure.
3. **Integrates the concepts of democracy, social justice and school reform through scholarship, dialogue and action.**	Separates democracy and social justice from guiding vision and accepts school improvement (a subset of school reform) as the dominant perspective.
4. **Operates from a deep understanding of ethical decision-making in the context of a dynamic, inclusive, democratic vision.**	Operates largely from perspective of the ethic of justice wherein obedience to authority and current regulations is largely unquestioned despite one's own misgivings.
5. **Sees one's career as a calling and has a well-developed sense of mission toward democratic social improvement that cuts across political, national, class, gender, racial, ethnic, and religious boundaries.**	Sees one' career in terms of specific job titles with an aim to move to ever greater positions of perceived power within the current system's structure.

In each of the five areas, the New DEEL leader is someone who sets off in a different, more challenging, and, hopefully, more rewarding direction.

The first vision statement challenges the notion of accountability squarely. Rather than being held to a system's accountability standards, we believe that educators need to be animated by an internal sense of responsibility to students, families, and the wider community. New DEEL leaders cannot focus solely on gaining better scores on standardized tests. Nor can they believe that making adequate yearly progress (AYP) is a route to a more just society. We consider responsibility to be a more authentic, more demanding, yet more satisfying approach to leadership.

Vision statement 2 encourages leaders to act in democratic ways to help develop young people. This means understanding how turbulence works

(Gross, 1998, 2004b, 2014b; Shapiro & Gross, 2013) and finding ways to protect those they work with from its excesses. In contrast, the traditional leader is a small part of a hierarchy that places constant demands and expects compliance. Members of the New DEEL feel strongly that the former models democracy, while the latter exhibits authoritarian behaviors that undermine the school's attempt to educate for democratic life.

Vision statement 3 speaks to the need for a coherent perspective that connects, rather than atomizes, the values of democracy, social justice, and school reform while encouraging dialogue and high-quality scholarship. We consider the three to be mutually reinforcing and inclusive.

A major element of New DEEL scholarship comes in vision statement 4—that is, the work of learning and practicing ethical decision-making from a multidimensional paradigm. New DEEL leaders understand that the ethic of justice, encompassing laws, rights, rules, and even guidelines, is important because it tells us what statutes and laws have to say on a given matter. But there are other ethics to consider in making important decisions. For example, there is also the ethic of critique that asks: Who made the law and in whose best interest? The ethic of care does not take notice of the law at all. Instead it asks: Who may benefit or be hurt by my decision? What are the likely long-term effects upon different people? Finally, the ethic of the profession takes into account professional ethics from different appropriate organizations as well as one's own code of ethics, both personal and professional. Above all, it asks: What is in the best interests of the student? Stopping with the ethic of justice will not suffice (Shapiro & Stefkovich, 2011; Starratt, 1994).

Finally, vision statement 5 deepens the discussion of being an educator from merely holding a job to a lifelong calling. Members of the New DEEL believe that this is essential, because only that kind of commitment will energize leaders sufficiently to transform our current system. Equally, seeing education as a *calling* honors the energy and sacrifice that these individuals have made.

We caution readers that Table 1.1 should not be read as a rigid dichotomy between good and evil. The New DEEL Vision Statement for Educational Leadership is a living conceptual construct. By that we mean that it needs to be amended and allowed to evolve with changing circumstances and deeper reflection. For instance, certain groups were not mentioned in earlier versions, including higher education faculty and staff members. Perhaps even more significantly, we now believe that there are problems with having the vision statement divided in two parts and leaving it at that. People are not either/or; they are mainly somewhere in between. This came up during a discussion in Joan's ethics class and caused us both to think a lot. Partly in response, Steve fashioned a large part of an education reform class to work with students to expand the ground in between the

New DEEL values and what are called conventional leadership behaviors. We do not support the idea that the middle ground is comprised of stages, nor do we believe that it is a smooth, linear path. People can and do move toward the New DEEL vision, but all of us sometimes drift back when conditions change. While this is not a neat process, it is a rich one that we explore in this book and will likely continue to explore in the years ahead.

THE ORGANIZATION OF THIS BOOK

This book flows directly from our mission and the scholarship our New DEEL community has done over the past decade (Branson & Gross, 2014; Normore, 2008; Shapiro & Stefkovich, 2011; Shapiro & Gross, 2013; Starratt, 2004; Storey, 2011; Woods, 2011). We drafted the title, *Democratic Ethical Educational Leadership: Reclaiming School Reform,* carefully because we wanted it to reflect the spirit of our efforts with strength and clarity. We believe that democratic ethical educational leadership is not only possible, but that it is needed if we are to redirect the very concept of school reform toward more humane and authentic priorities.

The structure of the book is also deeply imbedded in our values, because it is organized into five parts, each dedicated to one of the five New DEEL visions for leadership described in Table 1.1. The introduction to each part itself posed the challenge of detailing what that statement meant in practice so that the stories that followed would cohere. It is one thing to ask that leaders should be guided by an inner sense of responsibility to students, families, the community, and social development on a world scale (vision statement 1), for instance, but it is quite another to describe the implications and provide meaningful context for such an idea.

For each of the five New DEEL vision statements, we have solicited chapters from a wonderfully diverse group of educators. Each of these chapters depicts the experience of someone who embodies the qualities of that vision statement and is, therefore, an exemplar. The use of exemplars is also part of our practice, first started in the "Profiles of Democratic Ethical Leadership" course described earlier in this chapter. We believe in this approach because we see a need to tie critical concepts to the lives of real people. Without such a connection, principles such as the New DEEL vision may be seen as lofty but unreachable. We also believe that the careful use of exemplars makes it clear that we are speaking of real characters, imperfect yet striving to lead under challenging circumstances. In this way, we hope to help readers more easily identify with the exemplars rather than hold them in awe. Put simply, our book is built upon exemplars that we hope inspire readers to become exemplars themselves. In each case, we have asked contributors to describe the story of their character as she/he faced a critical incident, because we wanted to learn from that turbulent circumstance in our pursuit to connect theory to practice.

At the end of each account, we have posed questions that connect key ideas to practice. We have used our work in Multiple Ethical Paradigms and Turbulence Theory (Gross, 2014b; Shapiro & Gross, 2013; Shapiro & Stefkovich, 2011) to frame many of the questions, because the exemplars are dealing with ethical decision-making in the context of critical incidents.

In Part I, we explore the idea of leading through an inner sense of responsibility rather than being driven by external pressures of mere accountability. It is our belief that taking responsibility for students, families, and social development on a broad scale requires greater commitment than only agreeing to follow the orders of a given hierarchy. We also contend that this type of responsibility-driven leadership is more relevant to the needs of today's students. The exemplars described in this part show that such an approach to leadership is possible.

Part II further defines the actions of the responsible leader by highlighting educators who build community through democratic activities. These leaders understand how to work with the turbulence surrounding them. At times, this means shielding their organizations from severe or extreme turbulence. At other times, this leads to the careful elevation of turbulence in order to promote needed change. Readers will discover cases in this part where the leader's boundaries are as wide as the world. This is in marked contrast to the conventional leader who too often finds him/herself trapped into being a functionary in a corporate structure.

But what kind of vision do these leaders pursue? In Part III, we seek to answer this question by illustrating examples of leaders who combine democracy, social justice, and school reform. While this perspective may seem a matter of common sense, we believe that the dominant approach separates these crucial concepts by its near obsession with a narrow kind of school reform typified by high-stakes testing and market forces strategies. Conventional policy leaders may pay lip service to democracy and social justice, but only as distant possible by-products. The democratic ethical leader combines these ideals through judicious use of scholarship, dialogue, and action. Exemplars in this part demonstrate how this is accomplished and sustained.

Part IV centers on critical decision-making as the exemplars struggle with ethical dilemmas. We contend that the ability to consider multiple ethical perspectives is central to effective leadership, because leaders at all levels are confronted with complex problems that do not admit to any simple response. Of course, the ethic of justice is important, but we believe that effective leaders need to go deeper than merely asking what the law says. Conventional leaders too often stop there, leading to decisions that too often fail the test of fairness. The exemplars that we highlight in this part understand that the ethic of justice must exist along with the ethics of care, critique, and the profession. These men and women demonstrate an ability to reflect upon each of these ethical paradigms in order to resolve the dilemmas confronting them. They accept the complexity of ethical decision-making and know how to share their thinking with others in their setting.

Part V includes exemplars that sum up the results of democratic ethical leadership as we understand it. Rather than settling on a narrow job title, we believe that our profession now demands leaders who see their work as *a calling*. The women and men whose cases are described in this part believe *a calling* is far from being an antiquated phrase; they see today's educational leadership as a critical facet of social improvement that recognizes no boundaries. These people are on a transcendent, uniting mission that is a deep element in their character.

The conclusion focuses on learning and teaching, so that those who want to work with aspiring New DEEL leaders can create innovative curriculum using diverse pedagogical approaches. This part deals with shared values, theories, and praxis. It provides guidance to instructors for the development of New DEEL courses. It offers approaches that will make New DEEL learning experiential, fostering student engagement. We also encourage instructors to go to our website, by googling New DEEL, to find examples of innovative curriculum and of scholarship.

For Parts I through V, we solicited chapters from a broad cross-section of internationally respected scholars, believing that there were indeed exemplars of each of the five areas of our New DEEL vision. Our hopes were high, but the results trumped them. We are deeply grateful to each of the authors. Their exemplar cases brought our theoretical constructs out of the realm of thought and into the world of real life, with all of its complexity.

Our aspirations for this book are as high as the principles that inspire us. It is our hope that readers will challenge themselves to reflect on their own practice and use these exemplars as inspiration. Given the pressures of today's policy environment, many readers may find themselves stuck in the position of conventional leadership. Our hope is that the cases in this text, combined with the questions we pose for each, will help these colleagues find intermediate steps that lead to a richer professional life and a greater sense of integrity.

We may be in an era of disturbing paradoxes combining the best and worst of times. Rather than being immobilized by these contending forces, we see a path of vision and community building. It is our highest hope that educators around the world will decide to take such a course, and that our book will make a contribution to that effort.

NOTES

1 Alfred North Whitehead observed, "Education is the acquisition of the art of the utilization of knowledge" (Whitehead, 1929, p. 4). The spirit of that quote seems an attractive alternative to the pursuit of becoming an ever more dependent customer, since it recasts reform into an organic process.
2 For a detailed account of the development of the New DEEL, please consult S.J. Gross and J.P. Shapiro (2014), Ethical responses to educational policies. In C.M. Branson and S.J. Gross (Eds.), *Handbook on ethical educational leadership* (pp. 352–369). New York: Routledge.

REFERENCES

Addams, J. (2002). *Democracy and social ethics.* Urbana: University of Illinois Press.
Aiken, J. (2002). The socialization of new principals: Another perspective on principal retention. *Educational Leadership Review, 3*(1), 32–40.
Begley, P. T. (Ed.). (1999). *Values and educational leadership.* Albany: State University of New York Press.
Begley, P. T., & Zaretsky, L. (2004). Democratic school leadership in Canada's public school systems: Professional value and social ethic. *Journal of Educational Administration, 42*(6), 640–655.
Berliner, D., & Biddle, B. J. (1995). *The manufactured crisis: Myths, fraud, and the attack on America's public schools.* New York: Perseus Books.
Boyd, W. L. (2000). The "R's of school reform" and the politics of reforming or replacing public schools. *Journal of Educational Change, 1*(3), 225–252.
Branson, C. M., & Gross, S. J. (Eds.). (2014). *Handbook on ethical educational leadership.* New York: Routledge.
Cook, B. W. (1999). *Eleanor Roosevelt. Volume 2: 1933–1938.* New York: Viking.
Counts, G. S. (1932). *Dare the schools build a new social order?* Carbondale: Southern Illinois University Press.
Davis, J. E. (2003). Early schooling and the achievement of African American males. *Urban Education, 38*(5), 515–537.
Deresiewicz, W. (2014). *Excellent sheep: The miseducation of the American elite and the way to a meaningful life.* New York: Free Press.
Dewey, J. (1900). *The school and society.* Chicago, IL: University of Chicago Press.
Gross, S. J. (1998). *Staying centered: Curriculum leadership in a turbulent era.* Alexandria, VA: Association for Supervision and Curriculum Development.
Gross, S. J. (2004a). Civic hands upon the land: Diverse patterns of social education and curriculum leadership in the civilian conservation corps and its analogues 1933–1942. In C. Woyshner, J. Watras, & M. Smith Crocco (Eds.), *Social education in the twentieth century: Curriculum and context for citizenship.* New York: Peter Lang Press.
Gross, S. J. (2004b). *Promises kept: Sustaining school and district leadership in a turbulent era.* Alexandria, VA: Association for Supervision and Curriculum Development.
Gross, S. J. (2009). (Re-)constructing a movement for social justice in our profession. In A. H. Normore (Ed.), *Leadership for social justice: Promoting equity and*

excellence through inquiry and reflective practice (pp. 257–266). Charlotte, NC: Information Age.

Gross, S. J. (2014a). Where's Houdini when you need him? Breaking out of the U.S. educational reform straightjacket to reclaim our democracy. *Journal of School Leadership, 24*, 1099–1124.

Gross, S. J. (2014b). Using turbulence theory to guide actions. In C. M. Branson & S. J. Gross (Eds.), *Handbook on ethical educational leadership* (pp. 246–262). New York: Routledge.

Gross, S. J., & Shapiro, J. P. (2005). Our new era requires a new DEEL: Towards democratic ethical educational leadership. *UCEA Review*, 1–4.

Kliebard, H. M. (1987). *The struggle for the American curriculum: 1893–1958*. Boston, MA: Routledge.

Koopman, O., Miel, A., & Misner, P. (1943). *Democracy in school administration*. New York: Appleton-Century.

Miron, G., Urschel, J. L., Mathis, W. J., & Tornquist, E. (2010). *Schools without diversity: Education management organizations, charter schools and the demographic stratification of the American school system*. Boulder, CO and Tempe, AZ: Education and the Public Interest Center and Education Policy Research Unit. Retrieved January 6, 2015, from http://epicpolicy.org/publication/schools-without-diversity

Normore, A. H. (Ed.). (2008). *Leadership for social justice: Promoting equity and excellence through inquiry and reflective practice*. Charlotte, NC: Information Age.

Ohanian, S. (1999). *One size fits few: The folly of educational standards*. Portsmouth, NH: Heinemann.

Ravitch, D. (2010). *The death and life of the great American school system. How testing and choice are undermining education*. New York: Basic Books.

Ravitch, D. (2013). *Reign of error*. New York: Alfred A. Knopf. (See chapter 16, "The Contradictions of Charters," pp. 156–179.)

Reitzug, U. C., & O'Hair, M. J. (2002). Tensions and struggles in moving toward a democratic school community. In G. Furman-Brown (Ed.), *School as community: From promise to practice*, pp. 119–142. Albany: State University of New York Press.

Sernak, K. (1998). *School leadership: Balancing power with caring*. New York: Teachers College Press.

Shapiro, H. S., & Purpel, D. E. (Eds.). (2004). *Critical social issues in American education: Democracy and meaning in a globalizing world* (3rd ed.). Mahwah, NJ: Lawrence Erlbaum Associates.

Shapiro, J. P., & Gross, S. J. (2013). *Ethical educational leadership in turbulent times: (Re)solving moral dilemmas* (2nd ed.). New York: Routledge.

Shapiro, J. P., & Stefkovich, J. A. (2011). *Ethical leadership and decision making in education: Applying theoretical perspective to complex dilemmas* (3rd edition). New York: Routledge.

Smith, H. W. (1929). *Women workers at the Bryn Mawr summer school*. New York: Affiliated Summer School for Women Workers in Industry and American Association for Adult Education.

Starratt, R. J. (1994). *Building an ethical school: A practical response to the moral crisis in schools*. Oxford: RoutledgeFalmer.

Starratt, R. J. (2004). *Ethical leadership*. San Francisco, CA: Jossey-Bass.

Storey, V. A. (2011). *New DEEL: An ethical framework for addressing common issues in Florida schools.* Palm Beach, FL: JAPSS Press.

Tutu, D. (2005). *God has a dream.* New York: Doubleday.

Webb, L., & McCarthy, M. C. (1998). Ella Flagg Young: Pioneer of democratic school administration. *Educational Administration Quarterly, 34*(2), 223–242.

Whitehead, A. N. (1929). *The aims of education.* New York: MacMillan.

Woods, P. A. (2011). *Transforming education policy: Shaping a democratic future.* Bristol, UK: Policy Press.

Young, M. D, Petersen, G. J., & Short, P. M. (2002). The complexity of substantive reform: A call for interdependence among key stakeholders. *Educational Administration Quarterly, 38*(2), 36–175.

PART **I**

RESPONSIBILITY

New DEEL Vision for Educational Leaders	Behavior of Conventional School Leaders
1. Guided by inner sense of **Responsibility to students, faculty-staff, families, the community and social development on a world scale.**	Driven by an externally pressured accountability to those above in the organizational/political hierarchy.

Each part of this book is organized by one of the New DEEL visions for educational leadership. Each of these vision statements stands in contrast to the conventional approach to leadership. In this case, we examine what it means to be guided by a sense of inner responsibility to students, families, the community, and social development. We believe that this motivation is more powerful and leads to deeper, more sustainable democratic ethical results than the more conventional framework, in which leaders are driven by external pressures of accountability to those above them in the organizational/political hierarchy.

But what does it mean to be guided by such an expansive sense of responsibility? In part, it relates to seeing connections between oneself and the wider world. Langston Hughes captured this perspective in his poem *Freedom's Plow*, where he wrote:

Thus the dream becomes not one man's dream alone,
But a community dream.
Not my world alone
But your world and my world
Belonging to all hands who build.
(Hughes, 1974, p. 291)

Moving from the narrow self, responsibility is shared just as the goal is shared, but in a broadly egalitarian sense that builds community and a wider sense of "us." In this way, all players have a right, even an obligation, to create and sponsor new ideas, including their mutual liberation. This arises from an awareness of our interdependence. In his autobiography *Long Walk to Freedom*, Nelson Mandela expands upon this theme:

> I am no more virtuous or self-sacrificing than the next man, but I found that I could not enjoy even the poor and limited freedoms I was allowed when I knew my people were not free. Freedom is indivisible; the chains on any one of my people were the chains on all of them, the chains on all of my people were the chains on me.
>
> (Mandela, 1995, p. 624)

This expanded perspective, based on responsibility's foundation of connectedness, eventually led Mandela to see that:

> The oppressor must be liberated just as surely as the oppressed . . . a man who takes away another man's freedom is a prisoner of hatred, he is locked behind the bars of prejudice and narrow mindedness. The oppressed and the oppressor alike are robbed of their humanity.
>
> (Mandela, 1995, p. 624)

So the responsibility taken on by one leader not only broadens the leader's own scope, it can be passed down to others living far away in different eras—as Maya Angelou relates in *His Day Is Done: A Tribute to Nelson Mandela*:

> Yet we, his inheritors,
> Will open the gates wider
> For reconciliation.
> And we will respond
> Generously to the cries
> Of the Blacks and Whites,
> Asians, Hispanics,
> The poor who live piteously
> On the floor of our planet.
> (Angelou, 2014, pp. 32–33)

In education, two cases of leaders being guided by an inner sense of responsibility come to mind. The first is that of Horace Mann, whose work in Massachusetts led to the creation of a public school system in that state that soon spread throughout the nation. The intensity with which Mann pursued his cause animated his life and started a revolution. This was a transformation not only in the way that Americans thought about their duty to educate the young, but also part of creating of a more inclusive, democratic community. Lawrence Cremin observed:

> His quest was for a public philosophy, a sense of community which might be shared by Americans of every variety and persuasion. His effort was to use education to fashion a new American character out of a maze of conflicting cultural traditions. And his tool was the common school.
>
> (Cremin, 1957, p. 8)

Of course, Mann's work in America related to advances elsewhere, as he saw firsthand on his visit to Prussia. Some of Europe's educational leaders are well known, such as Pestalozzi, Froebel, and later Maria Montessori. Others who assumed the responsibility for spreading educational opportunities are not so familiar in our time. Sweden's Anna Sandström (1854–1931), a reformer and powerful advocate for women's education, is one such person. Renowned or otherwise, these exemplars of the past remind us of the power that an inner sense of responsibility can play in changing the lives of school children, their families and the wider community.

The second example, the late Szeto Wah, is far more recent. Yet he is also someone who may be new to readers. Wah founded the Hong Kong Professional Teachers Union (PTU) and led successful teacher strikes in 1973. Under Wah's leadership, the union grew from 8,900 to over 82,000 members. Wah went on to establish the Hong Kong Democratic Party, serve in the Hong Kong legislature, and support democracy in Mainland China. His reputation grew over these years, and in 2002, Wah was given the honor of delivering the first address in the Albert Shanker Lecture Series. Underscoring the need to transcend the school's boundaries to serve the practical needs of members and their families, Wah told his audience about PTU's role in establishing co-ops, medical centers, dental clinics, bookstores, insurance services, and continuing education opportunities. But he saw these activities as more than simply bringing tangible benefits to union members. Rather, these were the products of teachers exercising their rights to organize—an act only possible in a democratic society. That democracy must never be taken for granted:

> Throughout my career, I have been guided by the understanding that democracy and freedom of association must be fiercely protected. Only in a democratic political system can human rights, freedom, and rule of law thrive.
>
> (Wah, 2002, p. 2)

Just like Mandela and Mann, Wah used his inner sense of responsibility to expand the horizon of his aspirations to the wider world. In so doing, he became the servant of those he might never see and the inspiration of more democratic and ethical possibilities:

> For myself, I would like to be able to say, as did the American thinker and writer of Common Sense, Thomas Paine, at the end of his life, "My whole life has been spent on doing something useful for society."
>
> (Wah, 2002, p. 18)

In contrast to the power of responsibility, the conventional approach—wherein external pressure is used to drive accountability to goals established by someone else or some other entity—seems weak. The authors believe that responsibility is not only more satisfying and more likely to lead to democratic ethical results; it is also the more demanding of the two. The exemplars in Part I clearly illustrate the power and breadth of responsibility in educational leadership.

In *Maintaining a Commitment to Democracy (in Spite of High-Stakes Standardized Testing)*, Donnan Stoicovy teaches us what a highly responsible elementary school principal can do to remind students, their families, and the wider community of the core purpose of education, even in the midst of external accountability pressures. When her school faced punitive action from her state department of education after narrowly missing standardized test target scores known as Adequate Yearly Progress, Stoicovy took the problem head-on by actively uniting the wider community while she helped teachers to remember their own worthiness.

Judith Aiken, Cynthia Gerstl-Pepin, and Jill Mattuck Tarule tell the story of an exemplary university leader in their chapter, *A Leader Who Embodied Ethics, Equitable Policies, and a Community of Care.* Susan Hasazi was a democratic ethical leader who fought and won many victories for children with disabilities. While the center of her work was at the institute that she founded at the University of Vermont, her work transcended institutional boundaries to alter special education policies in her state and practices around the U.S. Her work illustrates responsibility-in-action ranging from direct help to individual children to altering the national landscape.

Just as in the U.S., England has turned to a market-forces approach to school reform that emphasizes privatization and competition. While many of that nation's education stories in recent years reflect that neo-liberal agenda, Philip Woods relates a very different account in his chapter, *A Co-operative Response to Entrepreneurial and Competitive Pressures.* Rather than deferring to the dominant policy directions dictated from above, David Boston, head teacher of the Sir Thomas Boughey Secondary School in Staffordshire, England, decided that his school needed to rekindle the 19th-century English cooperative movement. At David Boston's school, cooperation, self-help, and self-responsibility became key values. Woods's chapter ties these qualities to democracy and ethical behavior.

In *The Transformational Leader as a Thought Criminal*, Fenwick English takes us to wartime Japan and the life of Tsunesaburo Makiguchi, a public school principal. Makiguchi emphasized student-centered approaches in the classroom and fought against the power of elites. He went so far as to challenge the then-axiomatic belief in the infallibility of the emperor. English makes a powerful connection between the responsible and ethical stand that Makiguchi took in the face of his own government's fascism, and the challenge educational leaders face today in responding to the authoritarian aspects of our own educational policies.

Each of these exemplars represents a facet of what it means to listen to one's inner sense of responsibility. These accounts illustrate the deeply democratic ethical approach and its sustained impact upon a school, its students, families, and the wider community. Together, they represent powerful examples that can give today's educators helpful direction as they reflect on their own responsibilities.

REFERENCES

Angelo, M. (2014). *His day is done: A Nelson Mandela tribute.* New York: Random House.

Cremin, L.A. (Ed.). (1957). The republic and the school: Horace Mann on the education of free men. New York: Teachers College Press.

Hughes, L. (1974). Freedom's plow. In *Selected poems of Langston Hughes.* New York: Vintage Books.

Mandela, N.R. (1995). *Long walk to freedom: The autobiography of Nelson Mandela.* Boston, MA: Back Bay Books.

Wah, S. (2002). *Hong Kong's labor movement and the experience of the Hong Kong Professional Teachers' Union.* Albert Shanker Lecture at the Albert Shanker Institute. Retrieved July 8, 2014, from http://shankerinstitute.org/Downloads/Szeto%20 lecture.pdf

Maintaining a Commitment to Democracy (in Spite of High-Stakes Standardized Testing)

Donnan Stoicovy

> *The essentials of a good society are a wise and healthy people and a supportive culture.*
> *All else is derivative. The renewal of this culture requires a democratic people.*
> —John I. Goodlad

We want students to know that regardless of their age, they are capable of using their voice and making a positive difference in their classroom, school, community, and the world. Their social development is at the core of our mission, as the civic engagement of our students is essential to the health of our democracy. It is very important that we never lose sight of these principles regardless of the academic and political pressure of the current accountability system. Making sure that our students are good human beings, who work hard to make a difference, is at the core of my purpose! We also seek to lead our various constituencies, in both formal and informal ways, to develop an expansive community-building perspective. We work hard to engage community members to help us define the essentials of their vision of an ideal school and of what makes good citizens. Our joint vision provides the framework that empowers us to strive to make our school a living democracy.

However, reality occasionally reaches up and grabs us by the throat. Our school was placed in "Warning" in 2010 because we only met 16 out of 17 targets as identified by Pennsylvania under the Elementary and Secondary Education Act (ESEA), having missed the one other target (IEP/Special Education Reading) by .255 points. Our immediate response was to protest and to write an appeal to the Pennsylvania Department of Education (PDE) with the support of the Director of Special Education in our district.

We later lost the appeal and were saddled with the label of "Warning," which I was assured would carry no consequences if we managed to bring ourselves out of it. There would be no need to develop an "Improvement Plan." If we did not make the Adequate Yearly Progress (AYP) target the following year, we would move into "School Improvement," and a plan for improvement would need to be developed.

After many restless nights through the PDE's appeal process, I remained steadfast in my resolve that my values and beliefs are central to my modus operandi and are essential for personal and professional balance. If I am not balanced, then our teachers will feel it, and consequently may not be balanced in their classrooms—ultimately rattling our students. It is important for me, as the lead learner, chief worrier, and biggest advocate, to understand when and how to shield my school from turbulence, as well as understand when and how to use turbulence to facilitate change as we try to come closer to our democratic vision.

Ethical decision-making entails care, justice, critique and profession as illustrated in Shapiro and Stefkovich's model (2011). My first priority was to engage the ethic of care by supporting each teacher with compassion and empathy when sharing the news. All professionals are conscientious and care deeply about the success of their students. This clearly would wear on each of them as they think through everything repeatedly and place the blame on themselves. Modeling the ethic of care to them hopefully will demonstrate that caring for students is one of the primary purposes of schooling, and that they need to feel cared for in order to reciprocate that caring. My conversations were delicate and relational for each. I spoke one-on-one rather than sending an email or announcing it at our upcoming in-service. I allowed them to express their disappointment and encouraged them to remember that such standardized testing is only one part of the equation. I asked them to reflect on their students and their successes as demonstrated in the other benchmarks and authentic assessments they used with the students. Growth from each of their perspectives was abundant. I reminded them that one high-stakes assessment did not demonstrate what they knew about their students. For several people who took it to heart, I had to check in on them numerous times and through conversations to demonstrate to them that what they were doing with their students was the right thing. They did not need to change their instruction. There would not be test-prep workbooks in our school! I assured them that the type of teaching and learning they were engaged in had my full support.

Having the conversation with our school community was next on the agenda. While the information had not reached the newspaper yet, it was coming and would be front and center as headline news. Knowing that it was better that our school community hear that information from me before it was published, I took great pains to develop a presentation for our pending Back to School Nights. On my shoulders was the responsibility of explaining something to our school community that, in reality, did not make sense to me. I was overwhelmed by the outpouring of encouragement from the school community. Aside from one parent who clearly would have liked to have a voucher for his child to attend a nonpublic school (not part of the landscape in our state), parents spoke, wrote, and sent emails recognizing that our school is a good school and that no designation from the state saying that we were in "Warning" would or should steer us from the course that we were on. They were almost unanimously supportive of the kinds of learning that were occurring in our school.

Next, "while the iron was hot," I brought our community together for a forum to talk about "The Purpose of Public Education: What Do We Want for Our Kids and Our Community?" Approximately 35 parents, students and teachers attended the forum. After priming them through some thought-provoking slides, I invited them to respond to the guiding question, "What kind of people do we want our children to become (personal characteristics, virtues, knowledge, skills, habits, values, etc.)?" I had offered the structure of having people work in groups of four, but they wanted to work as a whole group since we were not a large group. Their responses included such things as wanting children to be critical thinkers, problem-solvers, and kind and compassionate people. We stepped back from the conversation and made several observations:

1. That there was nothing about high-stakes standardized testing in the discussion,
2. That these were characteristics of a thoughtful citizenry, which our school has been committed to fostering,
3. That we wanted to have the same forum again in November with each of us committing to bring several people with us, and
4. That holding a similar session with students would find out what they wanted from our school.

We established another meeting for mid-November, and in the meantime had the same conversation with a group of 75 kindergarten through fifth-grade students. Not surprising to us, their responses were similar to the general community. We were impressed with their thoughtful conversation and the passion that the students demonstrated. We encouraged them to attend the next community forum later that month to talk further.

Our next meeting drew about 35 people, including some of the students that we had hoped would attend. With results of the earlier sessions, we asked if anything was missing and moved into determining action steps. We agreed to the following principles: (1) Democracy is fragile right now;

(2) As a school, we are trying to provide students with opportunities to use their voices; (3) None of us is as smart as all of us; and that (4) We need the right people and a critical mass. One parent volunteered to draft a statement to be distributed to the larger community.

Then, in late spring, we received word that the PDE officials changed their minds about schools in "Warning." We would need to write a plan for school improvement after all. With little time left to do it, I pulled our Children First team together (we refuse to call our team a "Data Team" since children have heads, hearts and souls, and since our discussions go deeper than data), wrote the document in two afternoons, and submitted it. Our plan was approved by PDE, though in the end we did not need to implement it because we met our targets for AYP for that year.

I continually speak to our school community about the fact that this system is a trap. Regardless of what we do, we will inevitably fail in the eyes of PDE and the U.S. Department of Education, because the targets of the No Child Left Behind Act are impossible to meet. We have one of two choices: We can either go down the path that they want us to take by narrowing the curriculum and only teaching what is tested (or at least what we think will be tested); or we can continue the route that we are on to ensure that our students leave us as good people who live and learn within a democracy, have a rich curriculum that provides everyone an equitable access to knowledge, and experience a nurturing pedagogy and opportunities to engage in stewardship through civic engagement and service learning (Goodlad, 2009). I encourage them to maintain the second choice; it provides for the continuation of democracy.

I am constantly reminded that our profession is a "calling" or, as a former superintendent reminded us, that we are engaged in mission work on a daily basis. Teaching has a well-developed sense of purpose that leads us toward democratic social improvement, and that cuts across political, national, class, gender, racial, ethnic and religious boundaries. It is my goal to keep my sights on that democratic target rather than on the other Pennsylvania/ESEA-conceived targets that are put in front of me. I find myself compelled to return to the opening quote from John Goodlad, "We are seeking to develop a wise and healthy people" (2009, p. 1).

NOTE: Since the time reflected in this chapter, the provisions of the No Child Left Behind Act has been replaced by Race To The Top (RTTT), which has dropped the AYP requirements and the 2014 requirements of all students being Proficient or Advanced. It has, however, added that student assessment scores and school scores will be used to evaluate teachers, principals and schools. Convoluted multi-tiered evaluation systems have been developed in many states with formulas that are complicated and place a lot of emphasis on the grade levels being tested, and still only target Reading (English Language Arts) and Math as the only subjects that are

required to be taught, as well as the implementation of the Common Core State Stan-
dards (CCSS), which some have alluded to as a continuing step towards a National
Curriculum. Many states are using the Teaching Standards Framework developed by
Charlotte Danielson, who has repeatedly stated that the scores of students should not
be used to evaluate teachers, principals and schools as part of the Framework that
she created.

Questions to Discuss:

1. Who was the exemplar or lead learner in this case? Was this person a transactional or transformative leader? Discuss.
2. What was the critical incident in this situation? Describe.
3. How did the lead learner deal with this incident? Which constituents played a role in her process?
4. Which ethics did the lead learner turn to for guidance?
5. Was the lead learner able to keep the turbulence level under control? If so, how did she do this?

REFERENCES

Goodlad, J. (2009, August 4). What Are Schools For? The Forum for Education and Democracy. Retrieved February 15, 2014, from http://forumforeducation.org/node/487

Shapiro, J.P., & Stefkovich, J.A. (2011). *Ethical leadership and decision making in education: Applying theoretical perspectives to complex dilemmas* (3rd ed.). New York: Routledge.

Chapter 3

A Leader Embodied Ethics, Equitable Policies, and a Community of Care

Judith Aiken, Cynthia Gerstl-Pepin, and Jill Mattuck Tarule[1]

> *Leaders spend most of their time learning how to do their work and helping other people learn how to do theirs, yet in the end, it is the quality and character of the leader that determine the performance and results.*
>
> —Frances Hesselbein

When we were sent the call for chapters to describe a New DEEL leader who integrates concepts of democracy, social justice and school reform, and dialog and action, our former colleague, Susan Hasazi, rose immediately in our minds. We were reminded by others who talked about leaders who work from an ethic of care, connection, and a sense of social responsibility and how these qualities defined Susan's leadership (Beck, 1994; Noddings, 1992; Shapiro & Stefkovich, 2001). Susan served for two decades as the director of the doctoral program in Educational Leadership and Policy Studies at the University of Vermont (UVM), and she made a lasting impact on the program. The three of us interacted with her in various capacities and from varying power positions: Jill worked with Susan when she was Dean of the college and later Associate Provost; Judith was mentored by Susan initially as an Assistant Professor and then through tenure, as a program coordinator, and as an Associate Dean; Cindy was recruited by Susan as an Assistant Professor, and was mentored also through tenure, as a program coordinator, and department chair.

As a way to sort through our collective experiences, the three of us met to have a conversation about Susan and her unique approach to leadership, and how it has inspired each of us. Our conversation reinforced our belief that Susan was a practical and democratic leader who modeled exemplary ethical characteristics, i.e., commitment to the common good, appreciating multiple perspectives, and courage (Gerstl-Pepin & Aiken, 2009, p. 409). In this chapter, we share the fruits of our combined reflections and focus on Susan's leadership approach, which led to a stunning accomplishment as she created, developed, funded, and implemented the National Institute for Leadership, Disability, and Children Placed At Risk (NILDSPAR)—an institute aimed at developing "school leaders with the skills and dispositions necessary for educating students with disabilities and those placed at risk" (NILDSPAR, 2014). This was only one of Susan's many accomplishments.

Susan's democratic ethical leadership is most visible in terms of her commitment to work on behalf of children at risk and with disabilities, and to change the policies, practices, and conditions within our educational institutions that most impacted these students and their families. Educational leaders, in particular those who serve as special education leaders, face continuous challenges related to policies, legal issues, professional tensions regarding teacher preparation, inadequate funding, and challenges to practices of inclusion. Susan took on all of these in her work. Susan's work truly transformed special education in our state and impacted the field of special education at the national level. Our discussion acknowledged that her focus on at-risk children and youth with disabilities, and the lives of their families, was "sincere and genuine"; and that any efforts to bring about positive changes for these children and their families rested upon the ability to change the hearts and minds of school leaders. This was what led Susan to the goal of forming the Institute: To foster school leaders who truly cared about children with disabilities. For Susan, this meant building equitable and just relationships within safe and trusting spaces where, as Nodding would say, "care can flourish" (Nodding, 1999, p. 16).

We see Susan's leadership style as having three discrete qualities: 1) engaging in practices that reflected her ethical values, 2) a relational style designed to imagine possibilities and create community and positive social outcomes, and 3) advocacy focused on shifting policy towards justice goals. In the next three sections, we discuss each of these facets of her leadership approach through her development of NILDSPAR. We conclude with a reflection on what Susan's leadership says about what it takes to sustain programs and institutes in higher education aimed at nurturing New DEEL commitments and principles.

EMBODYING CARING ETHICAL PRACTICES

Susan's work as the director of the doctoral program served as a leadership model that informed how she created the Institute. Key to her approach was her grounding in an ethic of care (Noddings, 1984, 1992). She created strong relationships with everyone around her—administrators, faculty, staff, students, and community members. For her, it was not just enough to care; the individuals around her had to feel cared for. Any one could stop by Susan's office, and she would immediately drop what she was doing and make you feel like you were the most important person in the world. She wasn't just saying she cared, but you *felt* she cared. Whatever your role, she wanted you to know she deeply cared about you as a person. For her, it was a way to make the world a better place. Just as students with disabilities and those at risk for school failure needed someone in their corner, Susan was motivated by the belief that everyone needed to feel cared for regardless of their political position or means.

Despite numerous challenges, Susan worked from a deep, ethical commitment and passion. She didn't get pulled away from her beliefs, nor did she discount others' beliefs; she used her ethical values, skillful dialogue, and enduring passions to help people to think differently about the field of special education.

Susan tackled the hard work of improving the lives of special needs children and their families. She was skillful at "the use of various types of political but ethical action to navigate difficult organizational contexts" (Lipman-Blumen, 1996, p. 17). Such actions when *"used ethically for the good of the whole community* . . . can be extremely effective" (ibid, italics original). Her relational approach was, "denatured Machiavellianism . . . a term for principled instrumental action . . . that uses the self and others ethically as the means to an end"(ibid).

CREATING RELATIONAL, CARING COMMUNITIES

The million dollars of funding for the Institute came from a relationship Susan had developed with a family with a special needs child who was not being served well by a school. It was brought to Susan's attention that the family was struggling, and she intervened. Engaging in relational leadership, she was able to get the family connected to individuals who could help them navigate the "terrain of public schools" —and, ultimately, got the child moved into a better circumstance. Money was not an issue for these parents, but they didn't have the knowledge about what to do. So Susan took it upon herself to help, with no hidden motive.

It was much later when Susan approached the family about funding the Institute. She did it because she felt it was the right thing to do, and she knew they would agree. She knew they now shared a commitment to helping families struggling with similar issues. And further, nobody could say no to Susan, because she was so very genuine and passionate!

Her creation of the Institute was guided by her sense of an ethical responsibility to work on behalf of students, families, and communities. She called on her strong relational skills to get the work done. Her commitment seemed almost spiritual, a passion, and a belief in working on behalf of children with disabilities who needed someone in their corner.

ADVOCATING FOR CARING POLICIES

The one thing that was clear to anyone who knew Susan was that she "walked the talk"; her ethics drove her actions, communication style, and desire to make change and improve policy. This firm base shaped her practice, including her scholarship, which revealed her astute ability to question policy. If the policy didn't make sense and hurt people, she wouldn't accept it. She'd find a way to change it. She wouldn't let "a stupid policy or procedure" that wasn't humane and ethical get in the way of doing what was right for children and their families. She'd figure out a way work around it, while at the same time respecting the dignity and worth of those with whom she needed to interact.

Starting the Institute provided a platform for Susan to advocate and recruit others to the idea, and to recognize and address perspectives that differed from hers. She stuck with getting it going despite various roadblocks. Notable among these roadblocks were particular university policies about titles and how people could be paid. Susan used positive deviance (Shields, 2009) to solve these problems; for example, she called it an "Institute" instead of a "Center" so it would gain approval, and she appointed Fellows instead of hiring part-time faculty or adjunct faculty— which served to both solve a hiring issue and present a title that conveyed greater respect for their work. One never had the sense that what Susan was doing was somehow self-serving in any way. Everything she undertook was clearly driven by her ethical commitment to improve the lives of children and families facing challenges.

When we think about the significant contributions she made, it was always about figuring out what was an unintelligent and uncaring policy and how to change it. She was an exemplary "positive deviant"—someone who sought to subvert an unfair system that assumes children with disabilities or limited economic resources are pathologies that need to be destroyed rather than being worthy of care and support (Shields, 2009). When Susan saw an unjust policy, she refused to be silent.

But that was only part of her. Having been in schools with children with disabilities, Susan also knew that teachers often feel like they are in a vacuum. Further, while leaders and teachers know how to work with the children, they often do not have a clue what life is like for the families. And when the families go into the schools, they have to navigate all the obstacles that get in the way of doing what is best for their kid. Susan saw this, and she decided that central to the Institute would be changing the hearts and minds of school leaders by helping them to understand what life was like for families who had children with special needs. She selected graduate student fellows in educational leadership from around the country, and each started his or her fellowship by spending a week living with a special needs family. All of the fellows reported the tremendous impact this had on their understanding of special needs families, having seen such things as, for example, the tremendous work involved just to get a meal on the table for dinner. That's what Susan could do—she could navigate barriers and do it with grace. She could create contexts that could change people's minds. She demonstrated informed action. She also knew how to go around the policy, or how to divert it, or how to help others see the fallacy in it. Her ethical belief in doing what was right took precedence over ineffective and uncaring policies.

CONCLUSION AND IMPLICATIONS

Susan had a national reputation. Often recruited for administrative positions, she always said, "No, it will take me away from the work that really matters." She stayed at UVM and in Vermont, and she was absolutely committed to the program and the Institute, and to improving policies and leadership programs in Vermont and across the country. And she maintained contacts across the U.S. As a result, when she wanted to undertake something like starting the Institute, she could engage and organize a rich community of like-minded professionals to join her in effective, informed, and ethical action.

One of the crucial pieces of learning we take from Susan is that as a leader, she realized that you could not be democratic all the time, especially if other people were not being ethical. This could create tension, and she recognized that. And she also recognized that this work could have a high emotional cost, but she was willing to pay it. To address these challenges, she always operated from the ethical, moral point of improving education, and this sustained her. She transformed special education in the state, and she transformed how we prepare principals in schools. So when we think about the idea of a transformational leader, for Susan, it was not about change for the sake of change; everything she did was to make life better for everyone.

Questions to Discuss:

1. Who was the outstanding higher education leader in this story? What were some of the characteristics that made her so unusual?
2. Was there a critical situation or situations in this case? Explain.

3. Which group of students and their families did this leader help? Discuss some of her accomplishments.

4. If you had to describe the kind of leader that she was, which ethics did she favor and why?

5. How did this higher education leader deal with turbulence in her organization? Describe.

NOTE

1 This chapter was an equal collaboration among the authors.

REFERENCES

Beck, L. G. (1994). *Reclaiming educational administration as a caring profession.* New York: Teachers College Press.

Gerstl-Pepin, C. I., & Aiken, J. (2009). Democratic educational leaders: Defining ethical leadership in a standardized context. *Journal of School Leadership, 19*(4), 406–444.

Lipmen-Blumen, J. (1996). *Connective leadership: Managing in a changing world.* New York: Oxford Press.

National Institute for Leadership, Disability, and Children Placed At Risk (NILD-SPAR). (2014). About the Institute. Retrieved from http://www.uvm.edu/nildspar/

Noddings, N. (1984). *Caring: A feminine approach to ethics and moral education.* Berkeley: University of California Press.

Noddings, N. (1992). *The challenge to care in schools: An alternative approach to education.* New York: Teachers College Press.

Shapiro, J. P., & Stefkovich, J. A. (2001). *Ethical leadership and decision-making in education: Applying theoretical perspectives to complex dilemmas.* Mahwah, NJ: Lawrence Erlbaum Associates.

Shields, C.M. (2009). Dialogic leadership for social justice: Overcoming pathologies of silence. *Educational Administrative Quarterly, 40*(1), 109–132.

Chapter 4

A Co-operative Response to Entrepreneurial and Competitive Pressures

Philip A. Woods

Is innovation in contemporary education inevitably subject to the private and business-orientated values of entrepreneurialism? A strong and increasingly pervasive discourse in educational policy advocates more entrepreneurial leadership that reflects the dynamism and individualistic 'can-do' culture associated with successful businesses in competitive markets (Woods, 2013). This sits uneasily with conceptions of education that see schooling as a public good promoting civic virtues and personal development in addition to intellectual learning and skills for living and employment. It poses a challenge for school leaders who value the ethics of collaboration and community rather than the self-centred goals of individual and organisational competition.

This challenge is ingrained in England's school system as a result of waves of reform since the late 1980s. A more market-like environment for schools has been created, with much official policy faith being placed in leaders who are entrepreneurial and can heroically transform schools. School success is judged by progress measured in terms of narrow performative criteria. Innovation to improve education is therefore bent towards achievement of better grades, and scores that are important for passing the performative tests by which schools are judged and that drive national inspections.

In 1994, David Boston became headteacher of Sir Thomas Boughey School in Staffordshire, England. His direction of change and innovation, however, was not to be in the direction of individualistic competition and enterprise. On the contrary, it was to create a path towards a very different model of social action and educational success, based on the values of co-operativism.

The Sir Thomas Boughey School is a state secondary school, taking students between 11 and 16 years of age. When David became headteacher, it was—in David's words—a 'tired school', with inadequate buildings, a mix of outstanding and poor departments, and an individualistic culture where staff did not work together but worked as individuals. There was an absence of aspiration in the local community, too. With the closure of coal mines in the 1960s, the local area had lost its traditional source of work.

How did David respond to the challenges all of this posed? One of the most significant factors influencing David's response was his own upbringing and experience, and his awareness of what was valuable in the principles he had been shown and experienced in his early life. He had roots in the co-operative movement. That movement had begun in the North West of England in the 19th century and grown to be a global phenomenon.[1] The radical intent of the co-operative movement was born of a revulsion against the injustices and inequalities of competitive capitalism. The early 'co-operators' developed a practical organisational model that enabled people to work with and for each other, rather than compete against each other. The model gives members of a co-operative organisation (such as a manufacturing organisation, a shop, a farm, a school or other service provider) a say in its running and, if it is profit-making, a share in its profits. Co-operativism is about taking the best aspects of living as a community and making these an everyday part of the life of the organisation—rather than treating people as units of labour to use, as 'buying machines' to separate from their cash, or competitors to defeat.

David remembers his grandmother being a fervent co-operator. She presented him with a book when he was young that explained how co-operativism is about enabling you to lead your own life, rather than looking for an organisation (a political party, a company or any other kind) to do this for you. With the demise of nonconformist churches that were once so important in the school's local community, David saw co-operativism as offering values that represented people's continuing aspirations to a sense of collective and mutual responsibility and to a common good.

More specifically, David saw that there was a need to take a values-led approach to school improvement that would bring people along with him and create the conditions for sustainable change. This was a challenge that worried David—developing a school that over the long term would foster enduring values in students, and not simply 'weigh' their success through tests, and would treat teachers with respect. At the time David was thinking about this problem, the 'Co-operative Values and Principles' had just been redefined by the International Co-operative Alliance. David describes this as a 'lightbulb' moment. Not only were the Principles relevant to how he wanted to work with people, but their international status also gave them credibility.

Co-operativist principles were, then, the foundation for changes that David developed within the school. The school adopted a specialism—business; but it was business espousing co-operative values, sponsored by the Co-operative Group.[2] As David described it: 'We have "co-operative" over the door; we're co-operative in our being'. The school is managed co-operatively, meaning that heads of department and staff are involved in discussions, including an annual staff conference, and they know where the school is going. Strong management is combined with initiatives typically being led by staff, including newly qualified teachers. These are more than instrumental techniques for achieving better grades. They are founded in a deep feeling for a philosophy that guides everyday action and decision-making. David describes being co-operative as making sure 'we work with each other to create things'. It is a philosophy of supporting each other. Another of the ways that this is put into practice is through a 'young co-operatives' scheme, which gives young people a practical introduction to ethical enterprise by helping them to set up and run their own businesses through a co-operative framework.

In 2010, David led the school in taking a further, radical step. Whilst remaining in the state sector and therefore continuing to be publicly funded, the school became a co-operative trust school. Being a co-operative trust school means that it has a formal constitution and set of arrangements that enshrine co-operative values and ensure that the school is ultimately accountable to its members. The school is based on a legal 'articles of association', which requires the school as a trust to ensure that, *inter alia*, the curriculum and ethos of the school

> will place an emphasis on, and include a commitment to students learning about, the Co-operative values of self-help, self responsibility, democracy, equality, equity, solidarity, honesty, openness, social responsibility and caring for others with the aim of encouraging all students to become better citizens.

Any interested person who falls into one of five categories can become a member of the trust by paying a £1 joining fee. The categories are staff (open to all staff currently employed at the school), parents (open to parents of pupils registered at the school), community (open to members of the community who feel they want to support the co-operative), students (open to all students enrolled at the school) and 'other groups'. David explains the trust this way:

> One of the essential differences between a co-operative type business and a PLC one is that each member of the co-operative only gets one vote regardless of how many shares they hold'. This is also true in our co-operative. Additionally every type of member is equal regardless of the category of their membership.

Members elect a forum to represent them and make recommendations to the school's trustees (which includes the headteacher and two trustees elected by the forum) and governors.[3]

By the time David stepped down from being headteacher in 2011, the school he had joined looked and felt very different. It was oversubscribed and more successful in terms of its national examination results: The proportion achieving the standard 5 GCSEs (General Certificate of Secondary Education) increased from less than 30% to 80%. But this, of course, is to see the transformation only in terms of the narrow performative criteria. What David had worked to create was a culture that drew its inspiration from values based in a feeling for community and showed that business and enterprise rooted in co-operative principles was a real and viable alternative. This is not to say that everything is perfect or worked out as planned.

A most important outcome of David's leadership, however, is a legacy anchored in institutional change. The school cannot be isolated from the turbulence of the policy environment and from competitive and instrumentalising pressures. The re-creation of the school as a trust, however, with articles of association embodying co-operative values, expresses a vision and forms a protective barrier that helps in combating these pressures. Others are now working within and with that legacy—members of the trust (staff, students, parents and others) who are encouraged by those values to give them meaning in the life of the school through their own collaborative efforts.

Questions to Discuss:

1. Why was David Boston, Head Teacher, considered to be an exemplar in this case?
2. When he first took charge, how did David Boston deal with this "tired school"?
3. Was there any critical incident in this particular case? If so, what was it?
4. What kind of ethical beliefs did David Boston exhibit? Did his beliefs permeate his school? Did his beliefs extend beyond the school? Discuss.
5. How did David Boston deal with any turbulence in his institution? Did he desire turbulence or not? If so, why? Explain.

NOTES

1 For more information, go to http://www.co-op.ac.uk.
2 The Co-operative Group is the UK's largest mutual business, owned by nearly eight million members. It runs food stores, pharmacies, farms, funeral services,

legal services and travel services. See http://www.co-operative.coop/corporate/aboutus/An-introduction/ (accessed January 13, 2014).
3 For more information, go to http://www.co-operative.stb.coop/ and http://www.sirthomasboughey.staffs.sch.uk/information/docs/ArticlesAssoc.pdf.

REFERENCE

Woods, P. A. (2013). Sense of purpose: Reconfiguring entrepreneurialism in public education. In C. L. Slater & S. Nelson (Eds.), *Understanding the principalship: An international guide to principal preparation.* Bingley, UK: Emerald.

Chapter 5

The Transformational Leader as a Thought Criminal

Fenwick W. English

Although humanitarian competition is not yet visible in the international arena, persons who have gained some level of insight are beginning to realize that the ultimate winners in the competition for survival are not necessarily the winners of the economic race. It is not difficult, then, to imagine that the next form of competition will be humanitarian in nature.

—Tsunesaburo Makiguchi (Goulah & Gebert, 2014, p. 10)

Few outside of Japan have ever heard of Tsunesaburo Makiguchi (1871–1944) in the context of a transformational educational leader. By any definition of transformational leadership, Makiguchi qualifies. Here are some qualities of an educational transformational leader that fit into the framework of this book:

- Is able to think outside the cultural context and goals of a government or a state for institutionalized schooling, and takes action to challenge those goals if they conflict with a larger humanitarian purpose;
- Develops a pedagogical approach that places students first as opposed to schooling content first and the student second. Such an approach sees education as an active process where the learner creates meaning from an interactive and respectful schooling context;
- Employs an approach to teaching that does not practice beliefs that sort students into "winners" and "losers";
- Lives as an example of democracy in action and the treatment of dissent within a democratic social structure.

Tsunesaburo Makiguchi died in 1944 at the age of 73 of severe malnutrition in a Japanese government prison, where he was imprisoned as a result of his writings and beliefs about education. He was classified by the government as a "thought criminal." He had been imprisoned for 16 months, of which he spent 500 days in solitary confinement (Ikeda, 2001, p. 25). The nature of his arrest was based on his opposition to the *Peace Preservation Law*, a piece of legislation originally passed in Japan in 1925. Among other things, the law prevented Japanese citizens from criticizing the "emperor system" in which the rulings of the emperor were to be accepted without question and with unhesitating obedience, because the emperor was a god and without error. The system was the cornerstone of Japanese militarism. Makiguchi had criticized some of the major assumptions of this law. Specifically, he asserted that the emperor was not without error; therefore, he was criticizing a system of education that eroded the military's iron grip not only on Japanese society as a whole, but on the schools to perpetuate that society specifically.

Before his arrest, Makiguchi was under intense surveillance by the Special Higher Police. The official record of his arrest and retention indicates that for 13 months, Makiguchi "had attended more than 240 small group discussion meetings of the organization he founded, the Soka Kyoikyu Gakkai" and "also had office hours once a week when members of the organization and their friends visited his home for guidance and encouragement" (Ito, 2014, p. 34).

Even after his arrest and confinement, he tried to argue with his captors during interrogation sessions about the false assumptions of the government's approach to schooling. He never abandoned his beliefs, and he paid for them with his life. Few educators have had their beliefs put to that kind of test.

Makiguchi was not a world-class philosopher. He did not hold a government position, and he did not teach at a university. Makiguchi was a public school principal. Between 1913 and 1932, he served as an elementary principal of five schools, several of which were located in exceptionally poor districts. Because he was an historic dissenter of the schooling doctrines of the Ministry of Education, he was frequently transferred. Later, because he refused to cater to the special interests of the most powerful families by providing for more favorable treatment for their children in his schools, he was forced to resign his position.

However, Makiguchi wrote voluminously, and he argued for "co-existence with nature" and "peace and global citizenship" (Ibrahim, 2014, p. 107). Many of his books are still in the process of being translated into English. His most famous work, and one which experts believe is perhaps the most enduring in education, was *The System of Value-Creating Pedagogy* (in 12 volumes). In this seminal work, Makiguchi argued for the empowerment of teachers and the centering of active student learning in the classroom. His idea was that the school and the curriculum become part of the process of creating value through dynamic interaction. The role of the teacher was not to pour in knowledge, but to draw out from the student firsthand experiences that would enable the student to become a lifelong learner. In other words, learning how to learn took precedence over the simple acquisition of knowledge.

Moreover, the ultimate goal of education was not the advancement of the state nor economic or military dominance in the world, but rather on an enriched life of happiness. And by happiness, Makiguchi did not mean self-indulgence and a preoccupation with materialistic acquisitions, but rather on the "capacity to create value in the face of life's inevitable trials" in which education becomes a "process of personal growth that benefits the self and society" (Goulah & Gebert, 2014, p. 14).

Makiguchi's approach to education serves as the foundation to the idea of global citizenship, in which the final arbiter of value is "whether something adds to or detracts from advances or hinders, the human condition" (Ikeda, 2001, p. 17).

DANGERS OF BEING A TRANSFORMATIONAL LEADER

While contemporary educators may look at Makiguchi's life and writing as an extreme example of a humanistic educator speaking out against a fascist regime as atypical, transformational leaders today face the same obstacles for thinking against the goals of education being military dominance and economic hegemony in a globally competitive race. These goals are commonly advanced by U.S. political parties, neo-conservative think tanks, and business organizations such as the U.S. Chamber of Commerce (see English, 2014).

Contemporary notions of educational reform such as the *No Child Left Behind Act* and the *Race to the Top Fund* require top-down authoritarian modes of management lashed very tightly to test scores as measures of effectiveness. In such a system, there is no place for happiness or the role of the student as anything less than an empty vessel to be filled, and the role of the teacher as the master purveyor of knowledge to be tested. When school principals are to be fired for failing to improve test score performance, there is no place for personal value creation.

One result of this approach to education reform is already visible, as described by Collier:

> students' view of education is strictly instrumental and credentialist. They regard the entire enterprise as a series of hoops they must jump through to obtain their 120 credits which they blindly view as an automatic licensure for adulthood and a good job, an increasingly problematic belief.
>
> (Collier, 2013, p. A13)

And the reforms being pushed today across the board are based on "the perennial impulse toward bureaucratic command and control solutions, such as standardized testing or standardized grade-point averages, [which] only leads in the direction of more credentialism" (Collier, 2013, p. A13).

Today, transformational leaders like Tsunesaburo Makiguchi will also suffer a form of solitary confinement as they become increasingly isolated from the mainstream. Bucking the trends against standardization, impersonalization, authoritarian forms of management against the orthodoxies being embraced by the U.S. Department of Education, state departments of education and the neo-conservative laws that are passed for the de-professionalization of teaching and educational leadership preparation in colleges of education, these actions are vivid reminders that the "thought police" are still present, albeit in different form than *Tekko Geppo*, the Japanese Secret Police which imprisoned Makiguchi in 1943.

Transformational leaders are still viewed as "thought criminals," and their approaches are treated by neo-conservatives as an obsolete form of soft managerial approaches. This treatment is also directed at schools that have not reduced the discrepancies revealed in test score comparisons based on class and race, despite a growing body of evidence that such discrepancies are not controlled by the school at all but by the larger inequalities in society as a whole (Condron, 2011; Sahlberg, 2011).

The dominant advocates for reform argue for a brand of "managerial tough love" that is based on a scorched earth approach to low test score performance, and the installation of a culture of fear that has already seen the emergence of national test score cheating scandals in Washington, D.C., Atlanta and El Paso (English, 2014).

The courage and foresight of a true transformational educational leader is worth examining closely. Tsunesaburo Makiguchi's influence is felt today worldwide as several nations have embraced his approach, including India and Brazil, as well as two universities (Soka University in Japan and Soka University of America) that have been founded on his principles of pedagogy and leadership.

Perhaps the best judge of whether leadership is transformational or not is the legacy of change for the public good, based on the principles of ethics centered on the values of humanity beyond nationalistic borders that connect all nations to one another. However, then as in Makiguchi's time, such thoughts can be dangerous to the career of a true transformational leader.

The first test is to be able to see beyond the narrow confines of one's culture and time, and to be able to assess the values and ends of the educational system in which one is embedded and employed. This stance requires not only reflective thinking, but *reflexive* thinking—the latter being an appraisal of how one is thinking about how one is thinking, and how it may influence one's perception of problems and solutions. Transformational leadership also depends heavily on courage to follow through on one's diagnosis into the world of action. In this respect, the life of Tsunesaburo Makiguchi is an inspirational example.

Questions to Discuss:

1. Why did the author choose to highlight Tsunesaburo Makiguchi as a transformative educational leader?
2. What kind of education did Tsunesaburo advocate for and practice in the schools that he led?
3. Were there any critical incidences in Tsunesaburo's life that might have helped to create the person he eventually became?
4. When was the turbulence level high for Tsunesaburo? How did he handle the situations?
5. What ethics did Tsunesaburo turn to in his actual practice and in his writings?

REFERENCES

Collier, G. L. (2013, December 27). We pretend to teach, they pretend to learn. *Wall Street Journal*, p. A13.

Condron, D. L. (2011). Egalitarianism and educational excellence: Compatible goals for affluent societies? *Educational Researcher, 40*(2), 47–55.

English, F. W. (2014). *Educational leadership in the age of greed.* Ypsilanti, MI: NCPEA Press.

Goulah, J., & Gebert, A. (2014). Tsunesaburo Makiguchi: Introduction to the man and his ideas. In J. Goulah & A. Gebert (Eds.), *Tsunesaburo Makiguchi (1871–1944): Educational philosophy in context* (pp. 5–22). London: Routledge.

Ibrahim, A. (2014). Media review. In J. Goulah & A. Gebert (Eds.), *Tsunesaburo Makiguchi (1871–1944): Educational philosophy in context* (pp. 104–109). London: Routledge.

Ikeda, D. (2001). *Soka education: A Buddhist vision for teachers, students and parents.* Santa Monica, CA: Middleway Press.

Ito, T. (2014). Reading resistance: The record of Tsunesaburo Makiguchi's interrogation by wartime Japan's "thought policy". In J. Goulah & A. Gebert (Eds.), *Tsunesaburo Makiguchi (1871–1944): Educational philosophy in context* (pp. 23–35). London: Routledge.

Sahlberg, P. (2011). *Finnish lessons.* New York: Teachers College Press.

PART II

COMMUNITY-BUILDING LEADERS AMIDST TURBULENCE

New DEEL Vision for Educational Leaders	Behavior of Conventional School Leaders
2. Leads from an expansive community-building perspective. A democratic actor who understands when and how to *shield* the school from turbulence and when and how to *use* turbulence to facilitate change.	Bound by the system and the physical building. A small part of a monolithic, more corporate structure.

Just as the first New DEEL vision for leaders emphasizes the need to break away from the narrow confines of the organizational hierarchy, the second vision for leaders expands upon the need to build community through creative leadership (Furman, 2004). This means bringing together two specific concepts: knowing how to be a democratic actor, and understanding how to work with the inevitable turbulence that comes with innovative leadership.

On the surface it may seem ironic to speak of the democratic actor as a novelty in school leadership. After all, the foundational idea of public schools was first to create a citizenry capable of sustaining a democratic society (De Tocqueville, 2003; Dewey, 1900; Dewey & Dewey, 1915; Dewey, 1916). Therefore, one could conclude that the leaders of an institution so charged would naturally model democratic behaviors. However, anyone familiar with school management knows that this has all too rarely been the case. One reason for this has been the tendency to follow the example of corporations in the education of school leaders for most of the past century (Cubberly, 1916; Counts, 1927; Callahan, 1962; Tyack & Cuban, 1995; Saltman, 2010). We believe that this leads to the conventional behaviors seen on the right-hand side of the table, namely a leader who is bound by the system and the physical building, and one who is a small part of a monolithic, more corporate structure. Currently, high-stakes testing tied to the Common Core State Standards (CCSS) pressures educators to conform to external commands as never before in the U.S. This kind of leader seems trapped in the role of an obedient manager. We believe that this is hardly an enviable situation for those who wish to engender democratic values to our youth. Given that the pressures to conform are so powerful, the alternative needs to be equally potent.

A democratic actor, on the other hand, trusts her/himself and the school community. This kind of a leader understands the institution and the wider world beyond its boundaries. Thinking and acting strategically matter a great deal to this leader, so having sharpened political skills and a sense of statecraft are important qualities. However, unlike the conventional leader, the goal is to create mutually beneficial alliances tied to a positive, compelling vision of the future rather than achieve a narrow, temporary advantage. This type of leader likewise uses that knowledge to expand participation in decision making throughout the school and school district. Because this leader understands that community building requires an ever-expanding definition of who belongs, the goal is to widen the circle of "us," making the organization ever more inclusive.[1] Finally, this leader does not need to be the sole source of good ideas. In fact, this leader welcomes challenges and relishes debate, because he/she knows that is the best way to discover new possibilities for the wider community.

We intentionally use "turbulence" in this case to refer to Turbulence Theory (Gross, 2014). The purpose of Turbulence Theory is to provide a way of working with the continuing fluctuations in organizations. First, like the turbulence that pilots learn about, there are four levels of turbulence: light, which is related to ongoing situations; moderate, which refers to more active tremors with a specific cause; severe, which relates to a temporary loss of control; and extreme, in which the entire enterprise is coming apart.

Further exploration uncovered three drivers of turbulence that can raise or lower the levels. *Positionality* refers to a driver where one is in relation to a given disturbance, both literally and figuratively. For instance, the same situation may appear very different to a person with many resources than it does to someone with few resources. *Cascading*, a second driver, sets turbulence in context. Events surrounding any given turbulence shape how we respond to that event. If a school has just been warned that it missed cutoff scores for the government's standardized test, and its highly respected principal has announced her retirement, and there is an impending teachers' strike, any new turbulent event will likely seem more turbulent given the cascade of recent disturbances to the school's equilibrium. Finally, there is the driver of *stability*. Imagine that two schools fail to pass their annual budgets and need to make adjustments before bringing their request for funds back to the community. The first school has never failed to pass a budget before, and it has a solid reputation for its excellent academic program and its careful handling of taxpayer funds. The second school has had a new principal in each of the past five years. It has not passed its budget on the first vote in over a decade, and there is a group of anxious parents forming to bring order to what they perceive to be a situation out of control. The stable reputation of the first school and the relatively unstable condition of the second school create different dynamics. The latter is likely leading to a more turbulent path ahead while the former likely has a less bumpy path as each school attempts to pass its budget. Each faces the same problem, but the difference in perceived stability creates a different circumstance.

Since positionality, cascading, and stability affect one another, leaders are advised to consider their combined impact on a given situation. An unstable organization seems more likely to face cascading problems, which in turn impact various people to different degrees depending upon their position. In addition, we believe that leaders at all levels need to understand that turbulence is not always something to avoid, especially when they want to support needed change. That is why this part of the vision statement asks leaders to shield their organizations when necessary, but to also know when to use turbulence to take advantage of an important opportunity. We believe that turbulence surrounds all of us all of the time at some level, like any force of nature. That is why we advocate the approach of working with turbulence rather than trying to control it.

Consider the case of Franklin Delano Roosevelt and his careful use of democratic behavior combined with a sophisticated understanding of how to work with turbulence as he and his team responded to the Great Depression during the first months of his presidency. As FDR took his oath of office in March 1933, the economic and social fabric of the U.S. seemed to be fraying badly. Banks across the nation were facing extreme turbulence as customers stormed their doors, wanting to withdraw their savings. But that was only one aspect of the crisis. Dislocated workers, once confident of their jobs and their future, also faced extreme turbulence as they struggled to find work without the aid of a social safety net. Across the U.S., people began to despair for their own future and for their country. Roosevelt's response was a work in progress rather than a perfectly conceived plan needing only linear implementation. FDR promised his audience action and vigorous experimentation in the face of the crisis.

What emerged from the famed 100 Days following the inauguration was a wonderful case study of this New DEEL vision for leadership (Badger, 2008). Roosevelt behaved like a democratic actor by bringing a new set of people into the government to set new policies. While never relinquishing his authority, FDR encouraged a great deal of debate and invention. In this way, he used the extreme turbulence of the depression as an opportunity to create a dramatically new and expanded role for the federal government (Leuchtenburg, 1963). The whole thrust of FDR's New Deal was to stabilize people's lives, regardless of their position, so that the cascade of economic and social crisis would abate—and thereby eventually lower the turbulence level to a moderate level. Social Security, agricultural security, the minimum wage, massive public works projects, and programs for unemployed youth were just some of the programs aimed at ameliorating the hardships faced by millions (Downey, 2009). Economists from the left and the right still debate the New Deal policies and their immediate impact on the economy. What seems far more certain is the spirit of hope that Roosevelt's New Deal programs gave to a forlorn country, allowing the nation to carry on until times improved.[2]

Roosevelt is a clear exemplar of a democratic actor working with the turbulence of his era. Yet we do not have to go as far as the White House to see such examples of this New DEEL vision in action. Each of the chapters in Part II highlight exemplars who are just as compelling in their own time and setting.

Susan H. Shapiro's chapter focuses on the director of an early childhood center, Tammy, who was an outstanding leader on 9/11/01. Tammy had already created a center of distributive leadership and had already included the community. On this terrible day, the community played important roles in evacuating the school, located near the World Trade Center. A parent convinced a bus driver to take the children and community members to Battery Park and then obtain a tugboat to Jersey City. Once across the river, Tammy used TV cameras to show the children to the parents so they would know their children were safe. An alumni parent provided a place for the children to stay overnight. The leader kept the turbulence level down by keeping everyone working. Because of her leadership, they had built community.

Lisa A. W. Kensler and Cynthia L. Uline describe financial turbulence as it affected a school district and explained how a superintendent, Dr. Curt Dietrich, managed to deal with the financial challenge. This district moved from being an energy hog to an energy star under his guidance. Dr. Dietrich's approach was not a bunker mentality; instead, he looked towards positive change. He hired a Manager of Energy and Operational Facilities—a new position. He created a new energy policy. He closed the building as much as possible to save energy, and some staff were allowed to take vacation time or have abbreviated lunches and extended work days. He created cost savings. Custodial staff helped educate others about the greening of the building. Students worked on energy projects. In 2013, his district was declared Energy Star Partner of the Year with a 30% reduction in energy. He also received a grant to save energy.

Peter Liesenfeld and William Frick's chapter is told from the perspective of the principal who began to develop a community school. The principal moved in this direction because of two critical incidences. One occurred when the principal could not help a student who needed counseling services. After calling many agencies, the principal realized that rules and regulations prohibited his student from obtaining the help he deserved. In another critical incident, the principal and a father tried to think of alternatives to help a teenager who was on the road to drugs and disaster. Unfortunately, they found out that the assistance needed could only happen if the young person wound up in jail. Based on these incidences, the principal began to create a true community school, offering diverse kinds of physical, social, and emotional supports to enhance learning.

Barbara DiToro introduces a music leader, Dean Jacob Horn, from the College of Music in a research university. Horn did his best to be an effective leader. Initially, he tried to make the college look better by moving warehouse boxes and file cabinets from the entrance of the building. He helped open the new chamber music hall that was threatened when the contractors declared bankruptcy. He also helped with outreach and provided some assistance to a program that worked with a community in poverty helping students to take music lessons. When faced with fixing up a hall or helping children obtain music lessons, Horn chose the latter. He also created a world music curriculum. Sometimes he shielded faculty from turbulence, and at other times he created it through changes that he thought were important.

NOTES

1 Expanding the circle of who is considered part of "us" is the most telling difference between democratic leaders and demagogues, who divide and rule by creating a narrow "us" versus an evil "them." Consider the case of the fascists of the 1930s or the violent racists such as the KKK in the U.S. in the 1960s.
2 Near the end of his life, President Roosevelt ramped up his vision for a just society by advocating what he called a Second Bill of Rights. These included such guarantees as health care for all Americans, something we still debate. Nonetheless, his pursuit of ever greater economic foundations for the average citizen is an example of Roosevelt's commitment to democratic action on a national scale. See Sunstein (2004) for a detailed account.

REFERENCES

Badger, A.J. (2008). *FDR: The first hundred days*. New York: Hill and Wang.
Callahan, R.E. (1962). *Education and the cult of efficiency*. Chicago, IL: University of Chicago Press.

Counts, G. S. (1927). *The social composition of boards of education: A study in the social control of public education.* Chicago, IL: University of Chicago Press.

Cubberly, E. P. (1916). *Public administration.* Boston, MA: Houghton Mifflin.

De Tocqueville, A. (2003). *Democracy in America.* London: Penguin Books.

Dewey, J. (1900). *The school and society.* Chicago, IL: University of Chicago Press.

Dewey, J. (1916). *Democracy and education.* New York: Free Press.

Dewey, J., & Dewey, E. (1915). *Schools of tomorrow.* New York: E. P. Dutton.

Downey, K. (2009). *The woman behind the new deal: The life of Frances Perkins, FDR's secretary of labor and his moral conscience.* New York: Nan A. Talese/Doubleday.

Furman, G. C. (2004). The ethic of community. *Journal of Educational Administration, 42,* 215–235.

Gross, S. J. (2014). Using turbulence theory to guide actions. In C. M. Branson & S. J. Gross (Eds.), *Handbook on ethical educational leadership* (pp. 246–262). New York: Routledge.

Leuchtenburg, W. E. (1963). *Franklin D. Roosevelt and the New Deal.* New York: Harper Colophon Books.

Saltman, K. J. (2010). *The gift of education: Public education and venture philanthropy.* New York: Palgrave Macmillan.

Sunstein, C. R. (2004). *The second bill of rights: FDR's unfinished revolution and why we need it more than ever.* New York: Basic Books.

Tyack, D., & Cuban, L. (1995). *Tinkering toward utopia.* Cambridge, MA: Harvard University Press.

Chapter 6

The Importance of Building Community

A Preschool Director's Experiences on 9/11/01[1]

Susan H. Shapiro

Leadership styles played a very important role on 9/11/01. The directors of early childhood centers relied heavily on their leadership styles to help guide them through a very turbulent day. This chapter focuses on Tammy, the Director of a preschool center so close to the World Trade Center you could see the reconstruction site from the preschool's windows.

Tammy is a Caucasian woman in her forties. Tammy is a distributive leader. Heller and Firestone (1995) equated distributive leadership to that of a team. They wrote: "The utility of the team idea is that it suggests that the work of performing functions need not be done by one person or even one role" (p. 82).

Tammy describes herself as a leader who respects and listens to staff. Tammy makes sure to get input about the job she does from the administrative team. She takes input seriously and is able to reflect on criticism, incorporating it into her portfolio of leadership strategies.

Tammy's school's mission statement talks of mutual respect and trust: "Our school is a safe, nurturing, compassionate, learning environment. Children, parents, and teachers are mutually respected and trusted." Parents are encouraged to be involved in the school and to help make decisions and give input. This last point is important, because it helped Tammy and her staff on 9/11/01: Both the school and the local community were involved throughout the ordeal of that day. What follows is Tammy's story told from her point of view.

TAMMY'S STORY

It started out like any other normal day. It was only the fourth day of the fall term. We heard the plane had struck the towers. We thought it was an accident, so it was still "business as usual." When the second plane hit the towers, we knew it was more deliberate.

We decided to call parents and tell them that we would be closing. As a community, we decided not to allow parents to take their children until they had settled down and had washed off any dust so as not to scare the children. A little later on, a father, who was a police officer, rushed into the school. He said, "It is bedlam out there. Stay here and I will come and get you when it's time to evacuate." We tried to keep a semblance of order despite not knowing what would happen next. We concentrated on what the children needed. We read stories, sang songs, kept active. The staff wanted to come up and use the phones and call their families, which we let them do. We grabbed the backpacks that we take for neighborhood walks and started putting emergency supplies into them. We lost electricity after the second tower fell. I could see the people running down the street. The smoke started to come, and I could see the windows shaking. The children were actually very compliant and helpful. The only time I remember the children crying and being very upset was after both towers fell, and we were in complete darkness. There were probably 20 seconds that it took a teacher to find some candles and start singing songs like happy birthday while we searched for other flashlights.

We thought we would go out of the exit closest to the water. I remembered telling people to go out, and all the people in the apartment complex were out there too. I thought: we have to stay together. At least they'll find us all in one place. It's then we realized that there was dust coming in from the lobby doors. I said, "Everybody come back into the classroom." Some people from the lobby wanted to come in. They wanted to get away from the front doors that were leaking all the dust. We had some blankets that we wet and put along the door so that the dust wouldn't come in.

We had a father who convinced a city bus driver to come and get us. By that time, we only had eight children left. We had started with 65. We also had a lot of people here that were connected to the apartment complex. A lot of people came into the school when the towers fell. We also had parents who came to pick up their children, but they didn't know where to go. When the bus came, there were about 50 of us. We drove down to Battery Park and we got on a tugboat and it took us over to Jersey City.

When we got to Jersey City, we were all ushered into a high school. I saw the television cameras that were there. "Let's get the word out to these television cameras." We said to the news people, "Shoot these children." On a normal day, I wouldn't expose the children to cameras because who knows who's watching. That day we wanted their parents to see them, to know that they were safe.

We had eight kids with us whose parents didn't know where we were. The cameras let us say: "Look, your children are safe, they're fine." One of our alumni parents took us to his family's house in a small town in Jersey to spend the night. It was the next afternoon when we discharged the last child, and we could let go then.

During 9/11/01, Tammy worked to keep the turbulence levels down in the school. According to Gross's Turbulence gauge, Tammy's turbulence level was Extreme, which is classified as overwhelming and could lead to the destruction of the school (Gross, 2014). Although Tammy felt an extreme or severe level of turbulence that day, she strived to keep the turbulence level moderate to low for the children, parents and school staff.

The way Tammy dealt with teachers, parents and the community in the past affected the manner in which she worked with these constituencies during this crisis. Hargreaves and Fink (2003) feel strongly that a leader cannot do everything alone in this multifaceted world. They also stressed that it is essential to be flexible and responsive to the needs of a number of individuals in organizations that simply cannot be achieved by one person. Listening to the voices of the staff, for example, made a positive difference for Tammy during the crisis. Maintaining a sense of calm among the children, parents and staff set a good tone, enabling Tammy to deal more easily with that tumultuous day.

According to Gross and Shapiro (2004), during a chaotic event the director may be feeling an extreme amount of turbulence while the children are aware of only a moderate amount of turmoil. Gross calls this concept *positionality*.

Tammy's positionality was extreme; and yet she worked on making sure the children's level of turbulence was kept as low as possible. Tammy's distributive leadership style allowed her to share the burdens of leadership and helped lower her own and the center's turbulence levels. Tammy seemed to readily embrace her distributive leadership role, which may be in part due to her gender. According to Loden (1985), "women prefer and tend to behave in terms of an alternative feminine leadership model characterized by cooperativeness, collaboration of managers and subordinates, lower control for the leader, and problem solving based on intuition and empathy as well as rationality" (Eagly & Johnson, 1990, p.1).

Tammy kept the staff's level of turbulence down by keeping them working. She felt that the more they were working, the less frightened they would be. She also allowed them access to the phones, so they were able to worry less about their families and pay more attention to the situation at hand.

Due to the previously set tone, staff worked hard to soothe the children. For example, Tammy and her staff kept the children calm by singing happy birthday after the power failed. She related to the children in a way they could understand and appreciate, making the lighting of candles something festive instead of frightening.

Parents also felt high levels of turbulence during 9/11/01. Tammy and her staff had to work to lower the level of turbulence by soothing the parents in order to keep the children calm. She did not allow parents to take their children until they had settled down and had washed off any dust so as not to scare the children. This process lowered the parents' levels of turbulence.

Tammy used distraction, prayer and reassurance to help reduce everyone's level of turbulence. She spoke with authority and yet comforted everyone during a very scary time. In a situation where extreme turbulence was present, it was paramount for Tammy to help lower that level. Even with the rapid pace of decision making that these cascading events caused, appropriate answers to the problems were discovered, and these solutions lowered the turbulence level.

Tammy relied on distributive leadership strategies to help lower the level of turbulence on 9/11/01 from extreme to as moderate as possible. While keeping the focus of her attention on calming the young children under her charge, with the assistance of the staff, Tammy comforted the parents as well as lowered the level of turbulence in their preschool center. Tammy seemed to realize that keeping the turbulence level lowered was one of the most important activities during that day, as it would be impossible to lead effectively during a time of panic and extreme-to-severe turbulence.

Above all, Tammy and her staff had built community. Parents helped by assisting in the evacuation effort through the use of buses and tugboats, and providing places to stay overnight. In turn, the school helped people in the community evacuate by opening up the school to those in the apartment complex and by inviting them to come along on the bus and the tugboat. The reciprocity between the school and community was powerful.

Overall, Tammy exhibited outstanding leadership qualities on a frightening and terrible day—not through heroics, but through distributive leadership. Tammy developed a positive community prior to the critical incident that enabled her to direct a successful evacuation effort and take into account the best interests of the children.

Questions to Discuss:

1. Why would Tammy be considered an exemplar in this case? Why was she so outstanding? Describe.
2. What leadership styles did this exemplar display?
3. What was the critical incident in this situation? Provide some details.
4. What kinds of ethics did the leader display? Did she seem to favor one kind of ethic over another? Discuss.

5. Above all, how did Tammy handle this extremely turbulent situation? How did she bring the level of turbulence down, not only for the children, but also for the adults?

NOTE

1 This chapter comes, in part, from S. H. Shapiro (2007).

REFERENCES

Eagly, A. & Johnson, B. (1990). Gender and leadership style: A meta-analysis. *Psychological Bulletin, 108*(2), 233–256.

Gross, S. J. (2014). Using turbulence theory to guide actions. In C. M. Branson & S. J. Gross (Eds.), *Handbook on ethical educational leadership* (pp. 246–262). New York: Routledge.

Gross, S. J., & Shapiro, J. P. (2004). Using multiple ethical paradigms and turbulence theory in response to administrative dilemmas. *International Studies in Educational Leadership, 32*(2), 47–62.

Hargreaves, A., & Fink, D. (2003, May). Sustaining leadership. *Phi Delta Kappan, 84*(9), 693–70.

Heller, M., & Firestone, W. (1995). Who's in charge here? Sources of leadership for change in eight schools [Special issue: Teacher leadership]. *Elementary School Journal, 96*(1), 65–86.

Loden, M. (1985). *Feminine leadership: How to succeed in business without being one of the boys.* New York: Times Books.

Shapiro, J. P., & Gross, S. J. (2007). *Ethical educational leadership in turbulent times: (Re) solving moral dilemmas.* Mahwah, NJ: Lawrence Erlbaum Associates.

Shapiro, S. H. (2007). *In the playdough trenches: Early childhood directors' experiences on 9/11/01* (Ed.D. thesis). New York: New York University School of Education.

Chapter 7

The Transformation of a School District From Energy Hog to Energy Star

Lisa A. W. Kensler and Cynthia L. Uline

Beginning in 2007, the financial turbulence of the Great Recession affected public schools across the United States; and for many schools, the challenge continues. During 2009, North Penn School District (NPSD) faced such turbulence, reflecting level three in Gross' Turbulence Theory (Gross, 1998). This turbulence threatened the capacity of NPSD to meet its financial obligations, pay teachers, and provide high-quality educational programming for its 12,500 students. The superintendent of the district, Dr. Curt Dietrich, faced a financial challenge "the magnitude of which was never before seen in this district." The downturn in tax revenues and per-pupil funding, combined with increases in health care costs, resulted in a significant budget shortfall. Rather than resigning himself to cuts in personnel and educational programs, Superintendent Dietrich asked himself if there might be other strategies for saving funds and weathering this crisis.

The story of NPSD's transformation from an energy hog to an Energy Star reflects Gross' recommended strategies for facing severe turbulence. Thus, this chapter tells North Penn's story through Gross' framework. According to this framework, leaders facing severe turbulence should: (1) avoid a bunker mentality, (2) focus on the stability of schools, (3) prepare for the birth of new possibilities and an altered organization, (4) prepare for personnel changes, (5) emphasize a deep process involving all segments of the community, and (6) rely upon on data rather than personal opinion (Gross, 1998, p. 133).

AVOID A BUNKER MENTALITY

The financial cuts kept coming, with less money from local, state, and federal sources. The numbers did not add up, and yet, approaching the crisis with a bunker mentality was an option that did not occur to Superintendent Dietrich. Dietrich's early experiences growing up on a dairy farm established lifelong values related to conservation and efficiency. As he grappled with the dire budget realities, he saw opportunities to create change that would be good for the budget and good for the planet. Now commonly accepted in the public lexicon, "Going Green" was a message well received by his community. Heeding the sense of urgency at local, national, and global levels, NPSD set out to do its part. The United States needed to reduce dependence on foreign oil. The planet's atmosphere needed less carbon dioxide. If everyone in the school district embraced the challenge of decreasing energy consumption, cost savings and carbon emissions reductions would be realized. Ownership of the idea would take time and patience. Rather than focus on the naysayers (and yes, there were a few), Superintendent Dietrich aligned his message with the school district's core mission and values.

FOCUS ON THE BASIC STABILITY OF SCHOOLS

According to Superintendent Dietrich, the core mission and values of NPSD "guide how we behave and make decisions. They shape the culture and define the character of our school district." Each cabinet meeting agenda began with a review of goals and examples of the core values in action. These conversations reinforced the fundamental stability of the district. The district's laser focus on teaching and learning framed the conversation around improving energy efficiency. This was not simply an initiative to "Go Green," but a critical strategy for redirecting funds away from building operations and into classrooms. Recouping these costs allowed the district to serve its core clientele—students—during these turbulent financial times.

PREPARE FOR THE BIRTH OF NEW POSSIBILITIES AND AN ALTERED ORGANIZATION

When facing turbulent times, organizations must be open to fundamental changes while staying true to their core values and mission. Superintendent Dietrich understood the importance of explicit policy for guiding decision making and behavior across the school district. He took the ideas to the school board and made his argument for investing in energy conservation. This investment would require an energy policy and a new job position: a Manager of Energy and Operational Facilities (Energy Manager). The energy policy was established in 2010, and an Energy Manager was hired in 2011. The energy policy established standards and accountability for energy conservation, and the Energy Manager spearheaded district-wide energy conservation work. Tracking and addressing energy usage across the district's 20 buildings—through behavior changes, retro commissioning, and operations—required a positional leader who had the knowledge, experience, and authority to guide the effort. The organizational structure changed to serve the energy conservation aims.

PREPARE FOR PERSONNEL CHANGES

Personnel changes do not always mean hiring and firing. Other than the hiring of an Energy Manager, Superintendent Dietrich held district personnel constant and focused on personnel expectations and schedules. Early in the energy conservation efforts, naysayers were convinced the district was already as energy efficient as possible. Some district members were concerned about hiring an Energy Manager during such tight economic times. Although no one sought to undermine the initiative outright, skepticism was a primary challenge. Rather than debating these skeptics, Superintendent Dietrich promoted the message of energy conservation while empowering the new Energy Manager and others to actively implement the new policy. He was convinced that measurable results would bring the resistors along. In addition, Dietrich addressed concerns relative to the policy's effect on individuals. For example, concerns about physical comfort were addressed by maintaining comfortable temperature ranges during building occupancy. Twelve-month staff members' holiday schedules were adjusted, allowing for closure of all buildings during the regularly scheduled winter holidays when students were out of school, but staff were not. Employees could either take vacation time or make up time through abbreviated lunches and/or extended workdays. This change fostered positive regard for the energy conservation program, while at the same time it was realizing significant cost savings.

EMPHASIZE A DEEP PROCESS INVOLVING ALL SEGMENTS OF THE COMMUNITY

North Penn School District's energy conservation initiative exemplifies the development of a democratic learning community (Kensler, 2012; Kensler, Caskie, Barber, & White, 2009; Uline, 1997; Uline, 1998; Uline & Posgai, 2001). Enactment of the energy management policy required engagement and cooperation at all levels of the system. For example, a grant-funded partnership with the Alliance to Save Energy provided educational programming, resources, and support for school-based energy teams made up of students, teachers, custodial staff, and administrators. Custodial staff became key members of the learning team, educating teachers and students about building management and conservation. Ideas for reducing consumption beyond the retro commissioning came from everyone on the team. Empowered students led the behavior change initiatives with energy patrols, websites, posters, recognition programs, and even reminders to teachers about turning off lights and computers. Administrators took pride in their school's progress, motivated by weekly reports that held them accountable for their individual building's energy usage.

FOCUS ON DATA RATHER THAN PERSONAL OPINIONS

North Penn School District was a goal-driven and data-rich system. Both quantitative and qualitative data were brought to the table for discussion and recognition (Earl, 2009). The district used SMART (specific, measurable, attainable, relevant, and time-bound) goals and tracked energy usage in near-real time. The Energy Manager took responsibility for tracking the data, developing reports, and responding quickly to aberrations in energy use. As schools met their initial goal of 75 on the Energy Star scale, recognition and celebrations followed, and the goal advanced to 90. North Penn School District was a 2013 Energy Star Partner of the Year, realizing a 30% reduction in energy use across its facilities and saving more than $1.1 million in utility costs. These savings allowed them to retain teachers and educational programming during severe economic turbulence.

If you are a leader facing turbulent times, your clarity around personal and organizational core values will reveal opportunities for transformation. According to Superintendent Dietrich:

> It is so critically important to know what you believe and to live that and to show that to people, genuinely, day in and day out. You know, a lot of times you have to hold yourself accountable . . . say to yourself, "What is being asked of me as a leader and why is this happening right now? What is the best way for me . . . to respond . . . to move the organization forward?"

Questions to Discuss:

1. Would you consider Dr. Curt Dietrich to be an excellent leader? Why or why not?
2. Did Dr. Dietrich have a particular leadership style? How would you describe his approach to dealing with a challenging situation? Did he manage to include community in his leadership style? If so, which communities?

3. Was there a critical incident that created problems for Dr. Dietrich? Describe.

4. What was the turbulence level when Dr. Dietrich had to deal with his district's problems? Did he create more turbulence or less? How did he do this?

5. What were Dr. Dietrich's core beliefs? What kinds of ethics (e.g., justice, care, critique, profession, or community) did he use?

REFERENCES

Earl, L. M. (2009). Leadership for evidence-informed conversations. In L. M. Earl & H. Timperley (Eds.), *Professional learning conversations: Challenges for using evidence for improvement* (pp. 43–52). New York: Routledge.

Gross, S. J. (1998). *Staying centered: Curriculum leadership in a turbulent era.* Alexandria, VA: Association for Supervision and Curriculum Development.

Kensler, L. A. (2012). Ecology, democracy, and green schools: An integrated framework. *Journal of School Leadership, 22*(4), 789–814.

Kensler, L.A.W., Caskie, G.I.L., Barber, M. E., & White, G. P. (2009). The ecology of democratic learning communities: Faculty trust and continuous learning in public middle schools. *Journal of School Leadership, 19*(6), 697–734. Uline, C. L. (1997). School architecture as a subject of inquiry. *Journal of School Leadership, 5,* 194–209.

Uline, C. L. (1998). Town meeting and community engagement. *Journal of School Leadership, 8,* 533–557.

Uline, C. L., & Posgai, J. (2001). Changing the character of the comprehensive high school. *Leading and Managing, 7,* 44–60.

Chapter 8

On Leadership for Community Schooling[1]

Peter V. Liesenfeld and William C. Frick

Breaking free from organizational boundaries of institutional mass school-ing has long been a focus of whole-school comprehensive reform. Edu-cators, advocates, politicians, and employers have initiated district-level systemic organizational improvement. Among school models and district strategies, one *approach*, community schools, stands at the forefront of promising practice and offers an example of the kinds of school structures and processes, along with leadership practices, that exemplify the vision of New DEEL.

Community schools are conceived, initiated, run, and sustained through broad, collaborative democratic processes that situate family and commu-nity leaders as New DEELers in addressing the needs of the whole child. Promoting community support within schools, or extended, full-service community schools (FSCS), uses community partnerships and emphasizes community collaboration, where the school becomes the delivery point for comprehensive youth development, working holistically with children in response to systemic disadvantage (*Children's Aid Society, 2013; Coalition for Community Schools, 2009, 2010; Cummings, Dyson, & Todd, 2011*, p. 130; *Dryfoos, 2005; Dryfoos & Maguire, 2002; Milliken, 2007*). In fact, Commu-nities In Schools (CIS, originally called Cities In Schools)—one of the earliest prototypes of what we describe here, and the most consistently successful model of a community school in this country—focuses on not simply delivering community services to schools, but rather ensuring those services are *integrated* student supports, as in the CIS model (ICF *International, 2010; Moore & Emig, 2014*).

Community schools operate in a spirit of "progressive universalism," with a philosophy that in "societies characterized by inequalities, what

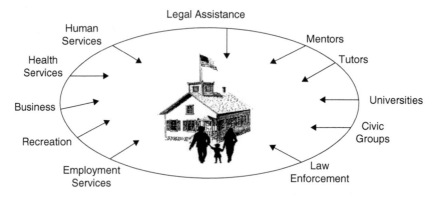

Figure 8.1 Community school as coordinated agency hub and delivery point for collective neighborhood uplift (illustration from Milliken, 2007).

is offered to all [can and should] be enhanced and intensified for those who currently have the least" (Cummings, Dyson, & Todd, 2011, p. 130). But legislative mandates, complex accountability structures, and shifts in requirements imposed on schools have obliged school leaders to focus on narrow performance criteria rather than a holistic approach to student development. Tenacity as a trait of school leadership in persistent nurturing of community schooling is indispensable for making the New DEEL vision transformative while effectively responding to pressures from local authority, community dynamics, and political mandates. Applying this philosophy requires partnerships of the entire community, and cannot be left to the school alone to implement and sustain.

In the following narrative, Peter Liesenfeld highlights critical moments reflecting these traits that have helped shape his current leadership role.

Some building leaders enter their positions embracing the New DEEL Vision for Leaders (Gross & Shapiro, 2009) either consciously or by instinct. My recognition of such essential principles developed out of a few critical moments in my career; in particular, two incidents changed my beliefs of the requirements of public education and fundamentally changed how I approached student learning and achievement.

As an administrator, one of my roles involved creating structures to facilitate student growth. My priorities became navigating accountability expectations, addressing local and state mandates, engaging in ongoing community relationships, and most importantly, facilitating growth of teachers as they grapple with the engagement of learners. In this transition, I became acutely aware of the complexities of teaching and learning in classroom environments. I realized my role was to help shield teachers from outside forces while striving to support them in other ways. My passion for students expanded to their families, as I realized those with limited access to system resources were often ill equipped to advocate effectively for themselves or their children. This became more evident as I spoke with teachers about the growth of students.

Teachers continually discussed roadblocks they faced in dealing with issues students brought with them to the classroom from home in order to focus on the learning at hand. Poor housing/living conditions, health issues, emotional conflicts, and unsatisfied basic needs plagued some students' families, and the ability of the teacher to engage the student while ignoring these issues inevitably failed. My reaction at first was that of many administrators: control what we can, ignore the rest. Teach students how to overcome regardless of obstacles, and persevere. We ignore the realities of life that students bring into the school building at their peril (and ultimately our own); doing so diminishes our ability as educators to fully explore a student's capacity for learning, and perpetuates a spiral of debilitating human and social capital suffocation.

By requiring students to develop multiple identities—the home-self and the school-self—educators undermine their ability to fully nurture student potential in a culturally aware and contextually sensitive manner. Consideration of all aspects of a student's life is essential in order to serve them. My understanding of our ethical responsibility to provide structures to serve families in supporting students in school and beyond, as we focused on learning in the classroom, came from two moments in my second year as assistant principal.

Most parents genuinely care about the educational experience of their children. The parents in my school spent countless hours in my office discussing issues with and about their children, and the difficulties of life circumstances they were faced with at home as they tried to support their children with their school work. They looked to me for answers, and I had none. I began searching for services and agencies to provide help, but I was met with bureaucratic hurdles that appeared insurmountable. A specific moment crystallized these frustrations as I sat with a family asking for help, and called a local counseling agency.

The parents recognized the need for counseling services. The student not only accepted the idea but was encouraged by the prospect of help. Upon calling the agency, I was informed that in order for services to begin, the parents had to come to the counseling office to fill out paperwork. The parents had no transportation and had only been able to get to the school because it was near their home. I asked the agency if someone could give the information over the phone and allow the counselor to come to the school to meet with the child. Due to liability issues, the agency representative explained to me, they could not initiate services over the phone; and since the counseling agency had not been approved through the central office of the school district, a counselor would be unable to come to the school. The conversation quickly ended with an apology from the agency that it would be unable to help the family.

I pride myself on my stubbornness, so I called six more agencies. Each agency, with slight variations, had approximately the same response: the agency was unable to help this student and family. I realized agencies outside the school were subject to similar regulations that schools are, but I found it unimaginable that in a city with such an abundance of community services available to help individuals, I could not find a way to bring help to this family.

The second critical event that led to embracing a model of community school within the public education setting occurred when a father entered my office, sat down on the couch next to my desk, and began crying as he described what had recently happened to his son. He explained that he had been asking for help for years: he had asked for counseling, an alternative school setting, anything to help him. He felt his son was on a destructive path leading to drugs and violence, and he had no idea how to help him. His greatest fear had now become a reality for him: his child had been charged with a grave felony, as a student in seventh grade. As shocked as I was to hear this, it grew worse as he continued. He had already met with the judge and district attorney, who had informed him that due to circumstances of the case, it would be dismissed and his son would be placed on probation for a year. When he explained the previous issues with his son, his inability to help his son, and his fear of what his son was becoming, the judge responded that there would be nothing the system could do to help until his son was in jail. As he wept, the father repeated that for his son to receive the help he needed, he would first have to be convicted of a crime, and end up in jail. He looked me in the eye, and asked me if I were him, what would I do to help my own son, rather than wait for him to end up in prison? All I could do was sit in silence, and cry with this father. I had no tangible answers.

These moments shaped my next years as an assistant principal, and eventually I moved to a head principal position at another school. Within my first three years here, our administrative team has closely examined the requirements of our job in light of our ethical responsibilities regarding the well-being and development of students in our building. Our long-term building goals shifted away from improving scores on state-mandated accountability exams, to focusing on the specific needs of each child. We restructured our schedule to allow for flexible interventions based on need, collaboration time for teachers, and additional time for students who needed additional supports beyond the class period. We developed portfolios for each child that incorporated growth in multiple areas, including efficacy, assessments, grades, attendance, behavior, trust, feelings of safety, and goals for the future.

By recognizing the needs of the community, as well as placing student needs at the center of our decision processes, we have begun forming a full-service health clinic, capable of providing care to students and families. This is the first step in our long-term goal to incorporate a variety of services in school to help students and families in the community. Considering our ethical responsibility to serve the needs of our students and families, the decision to create and sustain a community school was a necessary one. With such a disruptive change to the status quo, however, we expect a continuous stream of moderate turbulence as a result of these changes (Gross & Shapiro, 2009). Providing material, physical, social, and emotional support to enhance the learning environment—as well as to nurture social, cultural, and human capital development—compels us to continue through the turbulence that we expect.

Questions to Discuss:

1. Does the principal think of himself as an exemplar? If he does, why is this so? If not, why not?
2. What were the two critical incidences that the principal faced?
3. How did the principal and the teachers deal with the turbulence level? Were they able to create some calm in the school? If so, how did they accomplish this? If not, why not?
4. How would you describe the principal's leadership style?
5. Does ethic of community appear to be a priority for this principal? What other ethics are important to him? Discuss.

NOTE

1 This chapter is told from the perspective of Peter V. Liesenfeld assisted by William C. Frick acting as a critical friend.

REFERENCES

Children's Aid Society (n.d.). About Children's Aid. Retrieved March 27, 2013, from http://www.childrensaidsociety.org/aboutCoalition for Community Schools (2009). Community schools research brief 09. Retrieved February 2013 from http://www.communityschools.org/assets/1/AssetManager/CCS%20 Research%20Report2009.pdf

Coalition for Community Schools (2010, May). Community schools—results that turn around failing schools: Test scores, attendance, graduation and college-going rates. Retrieved February 2013 from http://www.communityschools.org/ assets/1/AssetManager/Turning_Around_Schools_CS_Results2.pdf

Cummings, C., & Dyson, A. (2011). *Beyond the school gates: Can full service and extended schools overcome disadvantage?* Oxford: Routledge.

Dryfoos, J. G., & Maguire, S. (2002). *Inside full-service community schools.* Thousand Oaks, CA: Corwin Press.

Dryfoos, J. (2005, Fall). Full-service community schools: A strategy—not a program. *New Directions for Youth Development, 107,* 7–14.

Gross, S. J., & Shapiro, J. P. (2009). Fear versus possibility: Why we need a new DEEL for our children's future. In H. S. Shapiro (Ed.). *Education and hope in troubled times: Visions of change for our children's world* (pp. 90–103). New York: Routledge.

ICF International. (2010). *Communities In Schools national evaluation: Five year executive summary.* Fairfax, VA: Author.

Milliken, B. (2007). *The last dropout: Stop the epidemic!* Carlsbad, CA: Hay House.

Moore, K. A., & Emig, C. (2014). *Integrated student supports: A summary of the evidence base for policymakers.* White Paper. Publication #2014–05. Bethesda, MD: Child Trends.

Chapter 9

How Turbulence Can Be Used to Shield or Facilitate Change

A Dean's Experience

Barbara S. Di Toro

Dr. Jacob Horn was dean of the College of Music at Eastern City University (ECU). Although he had joined the College of Music's choral faculty at ECU 20 years earlier, he had his first administrative experience running the college's outreach music program while still a doctoral candidate.

Throughout his administration, Dean Horn exhibited the same leadership behaviors that Peterson identified in effective principals (Peterson, 1999). In *The Instructional Leadership Toolbox*, Gupton summarizes that a principal with the leadership behaviors identified by Petersen provides instructional leadership and nurtures it in others, shapes the school culture and climate, manages and administers complex organizational processes, builds and maintains positive relations with parents and community, and leads and supports school improvement and change (Gupton, 2003, pp. 21–22). Dean Horn's combined teaching and administrative experiences during his postgraduate years helped him develop one more important skill—knowing when to shield members from turbulence (Gross, 1998, pp. 114–121) and when to use turbulence to facilitate change.

At the beginning of his administration, Dean Horn faced several challenges. He was confident that many of these challenges could be met without the majority of college or community members being aware of any turbulence, thus allowing them to proceed with their day-to-day business of teaching and learning (Gross, 1998, p. 14).

The main office of the College of Music had been serving as a warehouse for boxes and filing cabinets for over 30 years while staff and visitors made due with furniture long past its usefulness. Because this was an inherited problem, Horn determined that this issue needed to be brought to the attention of the provost. Agreeing with Dean Horn that increasing the efficiency and improving the physical appearance of the office were necessary, the provost approved a $15,000 increase to the college's budget.

The opening of the new chamber music hall, Clifton Hall, was threatened when the contractor declared bankruptcy just months prior to the new academic year. The contractor who had been hired by the university to do the renovation had left stairwells that were unsafe and the "fit and finish" process incomplete. The dean, along with internal facilities professionals, ensured that all safety issues were adequately resolved so that Clifton Hall would open only a few months behind schedule. Some of the trimming and touch-up painting would take place over the summer and between semesters. Very few people were ever aware of the problems behind the postponed opening of the much-needed chamber music hall.

Meanwhile, ECU's community outreach program, *Children's Music Scholars Program* (CMSP), was in jeopardy of being terminated. Initially established by the College of Education, the program had long served disadvantaged neighborhood children while providing graduate students with hands-on teaching opportunities. The program's mission was to provide financially needy children living in the neighborhoods surrounding ECU with music lessons, ensemble opportunities, and access to several free professional concerts. When the corporate grant that had funded the setup of the program expired, the university administration determined that the outreach music program should continue as a means of "giving back" to the community, but it delegated administrative duties to the College of Music's noncredit division, ECU Music Center. Now each nominated student was awarded a $500 scholarship towards lessons and ensemble opportunities. Their families were asked to contribute a small fee as a way not only to defray some of the cost, but also to improve attendance and boost commitment to the program. The combination of grants and the parents' contributions was barely sufficient to cover the cost of printed music and the additional faculty who were needed to supplement the graduate student teachers. The ECU Music Center's director, Mrs. Hood, soon secured grants from the National Education Association (NEA) and the state's Arts Council to further support this outreach program. Then, in midyear, a mandate went out from the top administration that all noncredit programs across the university, including ECU Music Center, would be self-supporting and required to return a small percentage of their income to the university. Failure to comply with the new regulations would result in termination of the offending noncredit program. It was evident to Director Hood that the delicate budgetary balance of the ECU Music Center was in danger of collapse, so she sought guidance from her immediate supervisor, Dean Horn. Together they looked for ways to increase income and trim the center's budget. Despite all their efforts, the budget still reflected a $15,000 deficit.

Dean Horn, being familiar with this program from his assistantship as its administrator, understood too well that many would be hurt by closing CMSP. The neighborhood community had come to rely on the program. Not only did it provide affordable music lessons and ensemble opportunities, but also parents felt that CMSP increased their children's chances to succeed in life. Many participants in the program became the first in their families to attend college. The college graduate students would lose a valuable teaching opportunity as well as be deprived of a service learning experience that would integrate meaningful community service with their course work (Jay, 2008, p. 255). The reputation of ECU would suffer the loss of a program that had long served as the university's goodwill ambassador to its neighbors (Di Toro, 2009, p. 141).

With other options expended, it seemed the only way to avoid closing CMSP was to approach the provost for a budget increase to cover the $15,000 shortfall. However, after presenting the reasons for the increased funds to the provost, Horn was reminded that the College of Music budget already had been increased to refurbish the main office. Another increase was out of the question. The dean would have to choose between the main office renovation or covering the CMSP deficit. Without hesitation, the dean made his decision—the children would come first. With the exception of the small administrative staff of the ECU Music Center and the Dean's Office, very few were ever aware that this long-standing service to the community was almost lost.

At a time when globalization was becoming a well-used buzz word (Osterhammel & Petersson, 2005, p. 8), the College of Music, which was part of a large urban research university, did not include world music in its curriculum. Horn strongly believed that to better prepare the university's music students for a global future, ethnological or world music needed to be part of the curriculum (Gross, 1998, p. 2). Horn met with the members of the curriculum committee to discuss how to remedy this deficiency and proposed adding a world music component to the curriculum, which would include adding new faculty to staff it. The dean reminded committee members that simply adding credits was not an option, as it would increase the financial burden placed upon students and inflate curricula. Widespread turbulence arose among faculty members who were concerned that their current teaching loads would be decreased or that the cost of hiring world music specialists would come out of their departments' budgets. Using turbulence to facilitate change (Gross, 2005), the dean guided and encouraged the faculty in finding ways to restructure the curriculum to better serve their students without any negative consequences for the faculty.

During his deanship, Dr. Horn often shielded his college community from turbulence that may have kept students and faculty from their primary purposes of learning and teaching. He was also aware that turbulence could be used effectively to bring about positive change. Essential to all of his decision making was a quality that would be the hallmark of his leadership style: "the best interest of the student at the center of all [of his] ethical decision making" (Shapiro & Stefkovich, 2005, p. 23). Perhaps it was in recognition of this student-centered administration that the provost eventually granted the funds needed to refurbish the main office of the College of Music.

Questions to Discuss:

1. Would you consider Dr. Jacob Horn to be an exemplar? If so, why? It not, why not?

2. What critical incidences did Dr. Horn face at the beginning of his administration? Describe.

3. What kind of leadership styles did Dr. Horn use? Were they appropriate for his college?

4. Regarding turbulence theory, did Dr. Horn use it well? Did he create more turbulence when appropriate and less when it was not needed? Discuss.

5. Turning to his ethics, what were Dr. Horn's priorities? Did he relate to the community? If so, could you describe his ethics? Did he focus on justice, care, critique, the profession, or community?

REFERENCES

Di Toro, B.S. (2009). *Non-credit community arts programs: A comparative case study of three programs within research universities* (Unpublished doctoral dissertation.) Temple University, Philadelphia, PA.

Gross, S. J. (2005, November). *Building the case for a New DEEL: Democratic-ethical educational leadership and the future of our profession.* Paper presented at UCEA Convention 2005, Nashville, TN. In S. J. Gross & J. P. Shapiro (2013), *Ethical leadership in turbulent times: (Re)solving moral dilemmas* (p. 172). New York: Routledge.

Gross, S.J. (1998). *Staying centered: Curriculum leadership in a turbulent era.* Alexandria, VA: Association for Supervision and Curriculum Development.

Gupton, S.L. (2003). *The instructional leadership toolbox: A handbook for improving practice.* Thousand Oaks, CA: Corwin Press, Inc.

Jay, G. (2008). Service learning, multiculturalism, and the pedagogies of difference. *Pedagogy 8*(2), 255–281. In National Task Force on Civil Learning and Democratic Engagement (2012), *A crucible moment: College learning and democracy's future* (p. 58). Washington, DC: Association of American Colleges and Universities. Retrieved January 12, 2014, from http://www.aacu.org/civic_learning/crucible/documents/crucible_508f.pdf

Osterhammel, J., & Petersson, N. P. (2005). *Globalization: A short history.* Princeton, NJ: Princeton University Press.

Peterson, K. (1999). The role of principal in successful schools. Reform talk of the comprehensive regional assistance center consortium-region. In Gupton, S. L. (2003), *The instructional leadership toolbox: a handbook for improving practice.* Thousand Oaks, CA: Corwin Press.

Shapiro, J. P., & Stefkovich, J. A. (2005). *Ethical leadership and decision making in education: Applying theoretical perspectives to complex dilemmas* (p. 25). Mahwah, NJ: Lawrence Erlbaum Associates.

PART III

DEMOCRACY, SOCIAL JUSTICE, AND SCHOOL REFORM

New DEEL Vision for Educational Leaders	Behavior of Conventional School Leaders
3. Integrates the concepts of democracy, social justice, and school reform through scholarship, dialogue, and action.	Separates democracy and social justice from guiding vision and accepts school improvement (a subset of school reform) as the dominant perspective.

Given the common rhetoric that schools are the foundations of democratic societies, it may seem unnecessary to assert the need for an integrated vision that connects democracy, social justice, and school reform. Yet deeper reflection on current educational policy in much of the world shows that a narrow emphasis on school improvement, often in the form of a single standardized test purporting to measure learning on a centrally organized curriculum, trumps almost every other aspiration for schools. While this trend has gained momentum over the past three decades, it is in conflict with a deeper tradition that joins democracy, social justice and school reform. We believe that vision needs to be reestablished.

We need only look at Horace Mann and the public school movement in 19th-century America to find clear evidence of this tradition (Mann, 1891). John Dewey (1900, 1916) furthered this connection between school life and the progress of the world beyond the school's walls. For Dewey and other Progressives, this required that children's education must be meaningful in the present, not merely as a step on the way to adulthood (Kliebard, 2004). Honoring the child's need for meaning is a further connection to democracy, school reform, and social justice, since it includes the learner, though young, as a participant in society rather than as an object to be manipulated by society. That perspective alone carries with it deep implications for the organization of schooling. Dewey's writings also emphasize the need for serious scholarship, questioning dominant educational policy priorities. Finally, Dewey is an exemplar of the academic engaged in public debate and action.

In a world struggling to recover from the horrors of the First World War and teetering towards the Great Depression, educators such as Harold Rugg of Teachers College focused on the kinds of curriculum that would fit so volatile an era. Rugg's *Man and His Changing Society* social studies curriculum texts were widely adopted even though they were often critical of social inequities (Rugg, 1929). Perhaps even more than Dewey, Rugg concentrated on the public's welfare and the possibility that formal study could improve social conditions. Similar series such as *Building America: Illustrated Studies on Modern Problems* (Department of Supervision and Curriculum Development, National Education Association, 1935) furthered this kind of exploration into social life.

In the same period, others worked directly with underserved groups in an effort to reform and democratize society as they reformed education. Hilda Worthington Smith and her colleagues famously pursued such a strategy at the Bryn Mawr Summer School for Women Workers from the 1920s to the 1930s (Smith, 1929; Heller, 1984, 1986). Many of the Bryn Mawr leaders and students came to prominence during the social reforms of FDR's New Deal, especially those promoted by Eleanor Roosevelt aimed at economic, social, and political equality for women. In the same era, Myles Horton established the Highlander Folk School in Monteagle, Tennessee. Originally working to educate area minors struggling to establish their rights (Smith, 2003), Horton went on to collaborate with such famous leaders as Martin Luther King Jr. in pursuit of nonviolent change for social justice (Adams & Horton, 1975).

Through the New Deal, the federal government itself became an innovator of just this kind of integration. Perhaps the most famous example would be the Civilian Conservation Corps, better known by its acronym CCC. Though limited by the social realities of pre–Civil Rights and pre–women's rights America, the CCC gave employment, educational opportunity, and social education to over 2.5 million young men from 1933–1942 (Gross, 2004); many of these young men were desperately poor (Uys, 1999). CCC camps were typically, though not always, segregated. Yet even with these limitations, African American participants were exposed to job training that was otherwise largely unavailable (Cole, 1999). Through the efforts of Eleanor Roosevelt, similar, though smaller, programs were established for young women workers (Cook, 1999). All of these efforts were aimed at hands-on, experiential learning as well as civic engagement in camp life.

As George Counts pondered the possibilities of schools themselves becoming the seats of massive social transformation (Counts, 1932), other educational leadership scholars began to create the democratic administration movement (Koopman, Miel, & Misner, 1943). The thrust of this movement, echoing earlier efforts to distribute school and district leadership by such pioneers as Ella Flagg Young (Webb & McCarthy, 1998), was to assert the power of democracy at a time of international peril. With the rise of Fascist Italy, Imperial Japan, and Nazi Germany, thinkers such as Koopman and Miel advocated democratic leadership at the school and district levels as an integral element to school reform.

More recently, the democratic school movement launched the Sudbury School (Greenberg, 2000) in the U.S. and the renowned story of Summer Hill (Neil, 1995) in the UK—two cases that demonstrate the possibilities, along with the possible limits, of democracy within the school community in daily practice. Clandfield (2010) depicted the power of school-community ties in Ontario that emphasize this kind of impact in a slightly different way. Begley and Zaretsky (2004) further described democratic school leadership in Canada and its potential. Gross (2001) analyzed a high school for newly arrived non–English speaking Americans. In this example, the school leader used a combination of democratic behaviors, innovation, and dialogue to steer the school around bureaucratic challenges. Finally, Woods (2011) introduced the concept of holistic democracy as a potentially comprehensive way to move forward creatively while engaging the whole community of learners, their families, and the wider community.

The four cases in Part III amplify these themes as they contextualize them in diverse current settings.

Bill Mathis discussed his experiences in helping to pass and implement education finance reform in Vermont that would create more equality of opportunities. He described how the bill was passed and his role in bringing it into fruition. The obstacles presented, after the bill's passage, from Republicans and wealthy critics were dramatic. There was a ferocious pushback. The fight was won but never finished. The 19th-century right to education was not accepted as a right. The tide had turned because of global competition, education as a market commodity, and parents who were denied consumer privileges. This was a state's move towards social justice.

Joe Polizzi's chapter describes the work of MindLeaps (formerly the Rebecca Davis Dance Company [RDDC]). Rebecca Davis had an outstanding education, with degrees in entrepreneurialism, international studies, and peacekeeping, as well as dance and choreography. She started to use dance to engage street children and underserved youths from postconflict and developing nations. She taught them about skill building, information technology, and health and water sanitation, and she developed retention, discipline, and cooperation among her pupils. She has worked in Rwanda, Guinea, Bosnia-Herzegovina, and the U.S.

Marc Brasof conducted a study of an innovative youth-adult governance model at Madison High School, a small, urban high school. The school was formed with a constitution similar to the U.S. federal government. Initially, the school was successful, with adults and students sharing leadership responsibilities. But three years later, there were problems with extreme budget cuts, teacher reassignments, and instructional changes. Students did not understand the system by that time. Larry, a student leader, and other student leaders asked the social studies teacher, Mrs. Santiago, to implement Active Citizenship units of study in all of her classes to build capacity for student engagement. Larry and a few students co-taught the unit with Mrs. Santiago. Students were to study a particular school program and draw up a proposal to be presented to school government officials. To illustrate civic participation, the students held a walk-out over the reduced funding for after-school activities and increased class size. Other schools joined, and they protested at the school district's central office. The students studied and worked on other problems. They also worked on fund raising. Larry and his peers developed increased student participation. Some funds were even reinstated after their protest.

Quisar Abdullah describes the leadership of a Muslim student, Daanaa Abdullah, who was born in the Carribean. He describes Daanaa's actions as president of Temple University's Muslim Student Association (MSA). Although very much wanting to serve democratically, Daanaa made two decisions that were unpopular. The first happened when Daanaa was traveling to a conference in Puerto Rico when the MSA student office on campus was broken into and items were stolen. One student was accused without proper proof. Daanaa saw this incident as the ethics of the community vs. individual rights and felt it was wrong to blame a student without evidence. In another instance, Daanaa was organizing a conference and realized that the MSA at the University of Pennsylvania (UPenn) was not included. He rectified the situation by asking UPenn to share the organization of the conference without letting the Temple University organizer know. He realized after the fact that this was not democratic or ethical behavior. Daanaa thought through his actions and learned from his mistakes. Profiting from experience is critical not only in this case but to the whole concept of democratic ethical leadership, since it allows for viewing ourselves as in process and avoids either/or thinking.

REFERENCES

Adams, F., & Horton, M. (1975). *Unearthing seeds of fire: The idea of highlander.* Winston-Salem, NC: John F. Blair.

Begley, P. T., & Zaretsky, L. (2004). Democratic school leadership in Canada's public school systems: Professional value and social ethic. *Journal of Educational Administration, 42*(6), 640–655.

Clandfield, D. (2010). The school as community hub: A public alternative to the neo-liberal threat to Ontario schools. *Our Schools/Our Selves, 19*(4), 7–74.

Cole, O. (1999). *The African American experience in the civilian conservation corps.* Gainesville: University of Florida Press.

Cook, B. W. (1999). *Eleanor Roosevelt: Volume2, the defining years, 1933–1938.* New York: Viking.

Counts, G. S. (1932). *Dare the schools build a new social order?* Carbondale: Southern Illinois University Press.

Department of Supervision and Curriculum Development, National Education Association. (1935). *Building of America: Illustrated studies on modern problems.* New York: Americana Corporation.

Dewey, J. (1900). *The school and society.* Chicago, IL: University of Chicago Press.

Dewey, J. (1916). *Democracy and education.* New York: Free Press.

Greenberg, D. (2000). *A clearer view: Insights into the Sudbury School model.* Framingham, MA: Sudbury Valley School Press.

Gross, S. J. (2001). Navigating a gale: Sustaining curriculum-instruction-assessment innovation in an urban high school for immigrants. *Journal of Research in Education, 11*(1), 74–87.

Gross, S. J. (2004). Civic hands upon the land: Diverse patterns of social education and curriculum leadership in the civilian conservation corps and its analogues 1933–1942. In C. Woyshner, J. Watras, & M. Smith Crocco (Eds.), *Social education in the twentieth century: curriculum and context for citizenship.* New York: Peter Lang Press.

Heller, R. R. (1984). Blue collars and blue stockings: The Bryn Mawr summer school for women workers 1921–1938. In J. Kornbluh & M. Fredrickson (Eds.), *Sisterhood and solidarity: workers education for women 1914–1984.* Philadelphia: Temple University Press.

Heller, R. R. (1986). *The women of summer: The Bryn Mawr summer school for women workers 1921–1938* (Unpublished doctoral dissertation). Rutgers University, New Brunswick, NJ.

Kliebard, H. M. (2004). *The struggle for the American curriculum: 1893–1958.* New York: RoutledgeFalmer.

Koopman, O., Miel, A., & Misner, P. (1943). *Democracy in school administration.* New York: Appleton-Century.

Mann, H. (1891). *Annual reports of the secretary of the board of education of Massachusetts for the years 1839–1844.* Boston: Lee and Shepard.

Neil, A. S. (1992). *Summerhill: A new view of childhood.* New York: St. Martin's Press.

Rugg, H. (1929). *Man and his changing society.* Boston, MA: Ginn.

Smith, A. (2003). *Myles Horton, Highlander Folk School, and the Wilder coal strike of 1932.* Archival manuscript retrieved August 29, 2014, from http://www.academia.

edu/174810/Myles_Horton_Highlander_Folk_School_and_the_Wilder_Coal_Strike_of_1932

Smith, H. W. (1929). *Women workers at the Bryn Mawr summer school.* New York: Affiliated Summer School for Women Workers in Industry and American Association for Adult Education.

Uys, E. L. (1999). *Riding the rails: Teenagers on the move during the Great Depression.* New York: TV Books.

Webb, L., & McCarthy, M. C. (1998). Ella Flagg Young: Pioneer of democratic school administration. *Educational Administration Quarterly, 34*(2), 223–242.

Woods, P. A. (2011). *Transforming education policy: Shaping a democratic future.* Bristol, UK: Policy Press.

Chapter 10

Sturm und Drang

Building "The Most Elegant Financing System in the Country"[1]

William J. Mathis

When equality in education finance reform was enacted in Vermont, author John Irving didn't call it "elegant." He called it a "Marxist plot." He found it "immoral" for rich folks to pay the same tax rate as poor folks. Further, he would not tolerate his children being subjected to "trailer-park envy." Irving proudly proclaimed he was an "unrelentingly elitist."[2]

Yet, an adequate and equitable school funding system is essential for equality of opportunity and, in turn, for a thriving democracy. Leaving aside political frothings, qualified and objective observers say Vermont has arguably the most equitable and adequate funding system in the nation.[3] But this achievement did not come easily—nor does it mean that it will remain that way.

Building this system involved a small number of core actors who came together at the right time and place. They included parents, lawyers, school board members, legislators and professional associations.

No one set out to be a hero. They simply recognized and embraced a great inequality, and they set about quietly doing their piece. Little praise was heaped on folks who took long drives on dark winter nights to address almost-empty auditoriums. I got involved when Ken Hood casually asked me if I wanted to teach school finance at the University of Vermont. So, I learned school finance the usual way—by teaching it. I ended up with a set of tools for examining equality and an understanding of the way funding formulas were built and implemented. This gave me insights into the struggle of towns unblessed with extensive property wealth.

I then turned to the tight discipline of 750-word op-ed pieces, explaining complex things in simple ways. These pieces, published statewide, resonated with a confluence of actors. Parents and citizens in poor towns needed relief from school property taxes. Members of the House Ways and

Means committee huddled near the statehouse, mooted solutions, and ran innumerable analyses. The state school boards association contributed the small amount of money that was needed. Everybody contributed their time, including the lead attorney, Bob Gensburg. This was not a big bankroll operation.

The preliminary work took years and was almost invisible. It was non-controversial because everybody agreed—in the abstract—that there was a problem. No one was paying much attention to this group of people who were sponsoring poorly attended public forums broadcast on public access channels. In retrospect, this lack of attention gave the actors time to develop their plans, analyses and skills.[4]

During earlier years, various reform proposals had passed the House and died in the Senate. Facing this reality, and with the knowledge of school funding decisions in other states, we knew we were inevitably headed to court. As a school superintendent, I recruited plaintiff school boards and the lead plaintiff, Amanda Brigham, along with her mother, Carol. By 1995, we had the legal foundations, plaintiffs and finance homework in place.

Then, things happened fast. It took only four months from the opening of the trial to a unanimous Supreme Court decision declaring the system unconstitutional. Only four more months were needed for the legislature to enact a comprehensive solution. At the Whiting School, Governor Howard Dean signed the Equal Educational Opportunities act into law in June 1997. Such a sweeping decision that completely transformed the state's finance system and tax system in such a short period of time was unprecedented.

I was to be the trial's lead-off witness until I got a telephone call the night before my appearance. A procedural motion had been filed contesting whether the state had the responsibility of ensuring equal education and equal taxation. The judge's partial summary judgment was quickly bumped-up to the Supreme Court, which unanimously ruled the state had ultimate responsibility. Once the state was found to be responsible, the issue was decided. Having all the legislative homework done ahead of time was key. The legislative work of Representatives Paul Cillo and John Freidin was absolutely essential—and they paid the price by being ousted in the next election.

To be sure, a small band of people transformed the state. But a perfect set of conditions also had an effect. The Senate had just turned from Republican to Democrat, and Howard Dean was governor. The state was coming out of a recession, but the tax pain memories guaranteed solid public support. The expanding economy paid for the reforms, and the national educational narrative favored equity and opportunity.[5] The top-down, test-based and punitive educational reform narrative had not yet taken hold.

But passing the law was only the beginning.

It was the ferocious pushback that came from the affluent ski towns and the Republican Party that resonated in this year of thunder. Folks in high-property-tax towns felt that all the property tax money was theirs—and they were not in a sharing mood. Senate Finance chair Cheryl Rivers had sold her old car only to see it being smashed with sledge hammers while parked in front of the statehouse. A nascent tax rebellion took place in 28 towns, and the retention of Supreme Court justices was challenged. This became part and parcel of the "Take Back Vermont" campaign, which saw conservative voices protesting what they saw as an over-reaching state.[6] As one commentator said, "It's the rebellion of the rich against the poor!"

What had been a relatively quiet undertaking had become the leading news story and the subject of howling letters to the editor and email exchanges. We had not signed up for a political war, but we were in one. This impassioned fervor led to numerous heavily attended forums around the state. Notably absent were most of the politicos. To be sure, Lieutenant Governor Doug Racine, Senator Rivers, and a few stalwarts would face the outraged citizenry. Also absent were representatives from the departments of Taxes and Education. As the politicians went to ground, an even smaller group led by former governor Phillip Hoff, Allen Gilbert, and me ending up speaking at a lot of these meetings. I escaped with only one punctured tire.

So what does this have to do with democratic ethical leadership? Sometimes you end up in an unexpected and fierce fight of principles. Sometimes you stand in an awfully lonely place, forlornly looking to the horizon, hoping the cavalry will come. Sometimes you wonder what's waiting in that dark parking lot a long ways from home. Sometimes the greater good of the society must take precedence.

Although that fight was won, in a sense, it is never over. The legislature's recent independent and positive report on the effectiveness of the act[7] is now met by people saying the formula is too old and confusing and needs replacing.[8] What drives this new energy is not the formula as much as the effects of federal cutbacks, a weak state economy, a decline in property values, and legislators' natural antipathy to the "tax" word. Unfortunately, the proposals now on the table would have the most adverse effects on poor and middle-income Vermonters.

Yet, there is a bigger threat. For most of the 20th century, education was the great democratizer, the engine of the American dream. In a time when the education narrative is shifting to being a global economic competitor, where education is merely a market commodity, and parents are effectively denied equitable consumer privileges, we must remember the Vermont Constitution's purpose of education is the nourishment of civic virtue and the prevention of vice.

The 19th century's enshrinement of the right to an education was predicated on the principle that education was too important to be politicized or subjected to erratic crosswinds. This exceptionalism of purpose is giving way to market models, privatization and the control of education by mayors, governors and the federal government.[9] The next set of challenges to democracy and to education is likely to be these very same forces, driving even greater inequalities of opportunity, a more greatly divided society, and the destruction of the American dream. Then a new band of leaders must arise.

Questions to Discuss:

1. Are there exemplars in this case? If so, who are they? What did they do to deserve to be called transformative leaders?
2. How did the exemplars exhibit leadership?
3. Was there a critical incident or incidents that led to them to take action?
4. What was the turbulence level throughout the passage and implementation of the Equal Educational Opportunities Law in Vermont? Did it change? If so, why?
5. What were the ethics involved by the exemplars as they worked on making the act into a reality? Did they lean more towards the ethic of justice, critique, care, profession or the community? Discuss.

NOTES

1 Statement of Governor Peter Shumlin. November 21, 2013. Reported in the *Rutland Herald*, November 22, 2013, p. B1.
2 *Burlington Free-Press* (June 12, 1998). John Irving on Act 60. See Irving's later explanation of his remarks at http://www.freerepublic.com/focus/f-news/1032399/posts
3 Picus, Lawrence *et al.* (January 4, 2012). An Evaluation of Vermont's School Funding System. Retrieved November 22, 2013, from http://www.leg.state.vt.us/jfo/Education%20RFP%20Page/Picus%20and%20Assoc%20VT%20Finance%20Study%20with%20Case%20Studies%201–2–12a.pdf. "Vermont School Funding System Works" (January 27, 2012). Retrieved November 22, 2013, from http://www.ruraledu.org/articles.php?id=2829.
4 Mathis, W.J. (2000, April). *Interest Group Influences in Advancing and Inhibiting Educational Finance Reform: The Politics of Equity in Vermont's Act 60.* Presented at the American Educational Research Association's annual meeting, New Orleans.
5 Honig, J.R. (2013). *The End of Exceptionalism in American Education.* Cambridge, MA: Harvard Education Press.
6 Mathis, *op. cit.*
7 Picus, *op cit.*
8 *Valley News* (November 19, 2013). Editorial: Battling Complexity; Vt. School Tax Remains a Challenge. Retrieved from http://www.vnews.com/home/9395851–95/editorial-battling-complexity-vt-school-tax-remains-a-challenge.
9 Honig, *op cit.*

Chapter 11

Rebecca Davis

Using the Arts to Make People Think and Remember Issues of Global Sustenance

Joseph A. Polizzi

> *It is important to point out that it is the leader's body and the way he or she uses it to express their 'true self' which is seemingly invisible mechanism through which authenticity is conveyed to others.*
>
> (Ladkin & Taylor, 2009)

Rebecca Davis is a classically trained ballerina and choreographer, and the founder and Executive Director of MindLeaps (formerly RDDC: Rebecca Davis Dance Company), an international, nonprofit organization based in New York City. She has studied dance since she was in elementary school, and she holds degrees in entrepreneurialism, international relations, and peacekeeping. She spent one essential but challenging year at the St. Petersburg Conservatory in Russia studying dance and choreography, which made a significant difference in the way she sees the world, motivates herself and her students, and is able to do the difficult yet joyful work she does.

Rebecca was motivated from a young age by actor parents to do well in school and to help others. While in high school, her involvement with Amnesty International informed her profound sensibilities toward social justice. The story of a Pakistani child laborer and youth activist, Iqbal Masih, who was later murdered, stirred Rebecca to create her first performance piece. In the piece, she delivered monologues and acted out the life of the child laborer on stage in front of her peers using speech, music, and dance. This experience laid the foundation for her study of the possibilities of didacticism through dance. In 2004, after graduating from Temple University, she was awarded a Fulbright scholarship to study choreography at the St. Petersburg Conservatory in Russia. It was here that she had an incident of lasting impression that affected her work ethic, resilience, and sensibilities.

As students and scholars of education and leadership, we are familiar with the culture of compliance that exists in schools. But, how does one succeed in this realm? In a culture of high standards and high stakes—not just for students, but for teachers and administrators alike—how does one meet those challenges head on? How can someone—a teacher, administrator, or student, thoroughly trained already in particular ways and practices, methods, and approaches that have been useful, effective, and informative—begin to learn another way entirely? This was the challenge that faced Rebecca when she was in Russia studying at the St. Petersburg Conservatory.

Russian ballet training is arguably considered to be the most physically demanding, rule-bound, and technically structured approach to ballet in the world. During Rebecca's time in St. Petersburg, she was challenged by the standards, the different system of learning, and the vastly different cultural norms and practices around her. It was physically challenging and brutal, with her commute being long, and her training being ten hours per day; the temperature was severely cold, and although she could speak and understand the language from previously studying abroad, *all* communication was in Russian. Her teacher was Nikolai Boyarchikov, the Russian *danseur noble* and director of the Mussorgsky Theatre, who was known for his talent in teaching the didactic ballet—the reason Rebecca had gone to Russia in the first place. But it was not the physical challenge nor the language barriers that were most difficult; it was the changing of a mindset, a framework, a lesson learned—and it has informed her global work. The most challenging aspect of pursuing her studies in Russia was described by Rebecca this way:

> Getting over the fact that you do not have the same creative freedom that you have here [in the U.S.]. That if you want to achieve something in that system, you have to conform. And as a very free thinker and a really independent and critical thinker, those are not skills that are valued there [in the Russian Conservatory], and until I got my mind around that, I said "I may have to conform if I want to learn the best of this system." I wasn't getting anywhere, and as soon as I got into that mode of thinking, I could really start to access the really wonderful teaching and coaching that they could offer me. But, you have to really be willing to assimilate while still keeping your core beliefs inside. And, I think that for American students that is really hard, because of these issues of individualism.
>
> (R. Davis, personal interview, April 2014)

For her final project, Rebecca wrote a libretto for a performance of Antigone. Because she was a talented American, Boyarchikov would not allow her to present and perform her piece; this was simply precedent and rules; no Americans had done so before Rebecca, and for this she felt an injustice. Using all of her Russian language skills, her strength of mind and character, Rebecca had to convince Boyarchikov, representing the Russian educational authority (which she had greatly respected), to allow her the opportunity to perform and be adjudicated as the other Russian students were. She was finally allowed to perform and received critical feedback that permanently strengthened her stamina. Rebecca saw being part of the final process as necessary to her growth and development. She was conscious of the connection or bond between herself and other people, seeing a deeper, more fundamental structuring of reality because of it (Korthagen, 2005). It was the moment where she realized that, for her to be able to learn in this different environment, it took something altogether different. She had been already trained in ways that had formulated her discipline, but in this new system she had to conform and adapt in order to be able to further her learning.

The American experience of education includes calls for a curriculum that emphasizes liberal studies for all students, but, it also calls for a curriculum that demands students be educated in ways relevant to their likely goals (Shapiro & Gross, 2013). Others, like Dewey, insist on a close connection between school and democratic life, and still others counter on rigid learning standards that are hierarchically imposed and undergirded by sanctions and reward (Shapiro & Gross, 2013). Rebecca's experiences epitomize all four of these approaches and ultimately enabled her to design and fortify the MindLeaps educational philosophy and program she has developed for the children she works with around the world.

Rebecca returned to the United States in 2005 and immediately founded and formed the Rebecca Davis Dance Company in Philadelphia (now "MindLeaps"). Armed with a new understanding of the didactic ballet, and a world-class resilience learned through toil, discipline, and trial, she was deeply motivated again to bring dance, history, literature, and social justice together as she had done at that performance in high school. The questions, "How can we make the arts about education, about learning?" and "How can we use the arts to make people think and remember issues of global sustenance?" informed her choreography in performances about the life of Helen Keller, the Enron scandal, and the Darfur genocide—all of which made people think and discuss issues on a deeper level. In 2010, Rebecca went through a transformation; knowing she was reaching an audience and was able to stimulate dialogue about important, difficult issues, she began to think about kids around the world who were not in school. She wanted to enact a more closely affective approach to using dance as a tool of democracy and social justice. Her idea was to use the structure and formality of teaching dance and the didactics of the discipline to be the foundation for school reform and to get kids into a classroom for study.

Today, Rebecca and her company teach dance around the world to engage the lives of street children and underserved youth in postconflict and developing countries. She runs a nongovernmental organization that uses a standardized dance curriculum along with a program to halt poverty. The organization does this by combining dance classes with skill-building and educational workshops in information technology, health, peacebuilding, and water sanitation, and other lessons that provide street kids an incentive to learn. The program provides a structure to develop cognitive skills like retention, discipline, focus, cooperation, collaboration, and motivation to prepare them for further academic study. Dance is used not only for performance or as a display of physical strength, technique, and discipline for entertainment and aesthetic purposes, but also as a means to educate, empower, and ultimately transform the lives of some of the most vulnerable and poorest kids around the world. In 2014, MindLeaps served 415 children in Rwanda and 680 worldwide (Rebecca Davis Dance Company, 2014).

All this work becomes dramatically clearer once you view or become involved with the various films, multimedia, and social platforms that Rebecca uses to educate, inform, inspire, enable, engage, and ultimately give voice to the street children and underserved youth around the world with whom she works. "Dance Up from the Street" (Goldsmid, 2013) is a documentary film that portrays the lives and hardships, successes and failures of the children in Rwanda with whom Rebecca teaches dance and educational skills. The Rebecca Davis Dance Company/MindLeaps YouTube Channel is easily accessible and displays the breadth and scope of the organization's international peacebuilding and conflict resolution work. RwandaYouth.com highlights the lives of children and offers blogs and other social media, along with ways to engage in dialogue and action with this community and to contribute. When we read and view the content from these sources, our imagination is stretched to the utmost, not, as in fiction, to imagine things which are not really there, but just to comprehend those things which are there (Feynman, 1965). In the films and other media transmissions, we can more clearly comprehend the lives of children and begin to understand what school reform looks like in the hardest places.

Rebecca Davis uses all of her skills to serve. She is a talented dancer, entrepreneur, and educator, a New DEEL leader whose educational approach considers the human condition as one of perpetual movement, progression, and change that leads to wisdom and action, eventually bringing clarity to the interpretation of life—both as an individual and collectively. She is an empathetic soul who holds at her core an integral understanding of the human condition, the interrelatedness of all living things, and, importantly, the connectedness of relearning the past in the context of the present to adapt and continue to work in service to others and a greater good (Polizzi & Frick, 2012). Rebecca Davis is effectively using dance to draw vulnerable and underserved children off the streets and into a classroom, where they are learning essential and fundamental life and academic skills.

WEBSITES AND MEDIA RESOURCES

www.mindleaps.org
www.rwandayouth.com
www.youtube.com/rebeccadavisdance.com
https://twitter.com/rddanceco
www.facebook.com/mindleaps
www.instagram.com/mindleaps

REFERENCES

Feynman, R. (1965). *The character of physical law*. New York: Modern Library.
Goldsmid, P. (2013). Dance up from the street [Documentary film]. China. CCTV retrievedfromhttp://english.cntv.cn/program/facesofafrica/20130506/103389.shtml
Korthagen, F. (2005). The organization in balance: Reflection and intuition as complementary processes. *Management Learning, 36*(3), 371–387.
Ladkin, D., & Taylor, S. (2009). Enacting the 'true self': Towards a theory of embodied authentic leadership. *Leadership Quarterly, 21*(1), 64–74. doi:10.1016/j.leaqua.2009.10.005
Polizzi, J. A., & Frick, W. (2012). Transformative preparation and professional development: Authentic reflective practice for school leadership. *Teaching and Learning: The Journal of Natural Inquiry and Reflective Practice, 26*(1), 20–34. Retrieved from http://works.bepress.com/joseph_polizzi/5 on 1/10/14
Rebecca Davis Dance Company. (2014). *Annual report 2013*. Retrieved from http://report2013.rebeccadavisdance.com/
Shapiro, J. P., & Gross, S. (2013). *Ethical educational leadership in turbulent times: (Re) solving moral dilemmas* (2nd ed.). New York: Routledge.

Chapter 12

Student Voice in School Reform

The Madison High School Youth Governance Model

Marc Brasof

> *[W]e change things but we are terrible at improving things . . . School spirit isn't going to happen until the school has a structure and curriculum capable of creating civic activism and critical thinking.*
>
> —Senior Larry, Speaker of the House of Students, aptly summarizing student research conclusions about school life to faculty leadership

A promising approach to fulfilling the New DEEL's vision of school transformation, where leaders integrate the concepts of democracy, social justice and school reform through scholarship, dialogue and action, is to include students into the policy creation, implementation and review process at the building level. Student leadership activity can range from 'being heard'—adults listening to students—to 'building the leadership capacity of the school'—students leading school improvement initiatives (Mitra, 2006). Does the inclusion of students in school reform conversations create more socially just, effective institutions?

YOUTH-ADULT PARTNERSHIPS IN SCHOOLS MATTER

At an organizational level, including voice in school reform has produced more democratic, socially just institutions (Cook-Sather, Cohen, & Alter, 2010; Fielding, 2001; Mitra, 2004; Zeldin, 2004a) and greatly improved the effectiveness and sustainability of institutions' projects and processes (Brasof, 2014; Ranjani, 2001). Students often had important insights into classroom learning and were more open than adults to discussing sensitive issues dealing with school culture, organizational structure, and overall school climate (Arnot & Reay, 2004, cited by Brasof, 2014; Fine, 1991; Johnston & Nicholls, 1995; Mitra 2003; Rudduck & McIntyre, 2007; Stevenson & Ellsworth, 1991; Wehlage et al., 1989). And student participation has improved organizational outcomes in other areas, such as student enrollment, family and community involvement, disciplinary incidents, student safety, class attendance, and graduation rates (Pekrul & Levin, 2007; Rudduck & McIntyre, 2007; Thomson & Holdsworth, 2003). Moreover, research has found students benefiting directly from being involved in school reform initiatives or organizational governance. Students developed a sense of equality, agency, belonging and a range of social and academic competencies (Camino, 2000; Cook-Sather, 2002, 2010; Dempster, 2006; Kaba, 2000/2001; Mitra, 2004; Rudduck, 2002, 2007; Rudduck & McIntyre, 2007; Zeldin, 2004a; Zeldin, Camino & Mook, 2005; Zeldin, McDaniel, Topitzes, & Calvert, 2000). A growing body of research clearly indicates that including students in school reform dialogue is creating more socially just and effective institutions.

MADISON HIGH SCHOOL: A CASE STUDY OF
YOUTH-ADULT LEADERSHIP

I conducted a recent study on an innovative youth-adult governance model at Madison High School (MHS),[1] an urban small public high school located in the northeast region of the United States. This study (Brasof, 2014) illustrated how schools can cultivate student leadership in order to improve schools.

Madison High School's school governance system is modeled after the federal government, containing an executive, bi-cameral legislature and a Supreme Court.[2] Students and faculty share responsibility for creating, implementing and reviewing school policy and practices through a system of separation of powers, checks and federalism. Over a seven-year period, faculty, students and administrators have used this system's constitutional mechanisms and other democratic practices to address a wide range of issues: developing the uniform code, maintaining the integrity of school elections, adjusting the school's operational hours, addressing an ineffective and inequitable lateness policy, organizing lunch time and expanding after-school activities.

While these efforts were successful at creating a productive school climate, over the next three years MHS began experiencing a series of internal challenges, some brought on by external forces (extreme budget cuts and teacher reassignments), while others were created from within (an increasingly divided instructional vision among faculty, leading to a contentious reorganization of the program of study). Together, these forces began to undermine the school climate, as evident in student disengagement in coursework across the school, student misbehavior becoming gradually more difficult to address, and faculty's low morale. In our interview, senior Larry, Speaker of the House of Students, described the school climate and sense of community: "[Everyone] is unhappy . . . It's the feeling around the school." It was the newly elected student government leaders' hopes to increase the school's sense of community and improve the overall school climate, a challenge they believed that writing legislation, an executive order, or a court case would be unable to achieve.

In addition, student leaders began to realize that the school's new generation of students and faculty did not understand the school's government structure and how to use their voice. As one student put it to student leaders during an after-school meeting:

> The founding class wrote a constitution for a reason. The reason is for us to use it and not to just let it sit there on the wall and look pretty . . . everyone is talking about writing bills like the lunch or uniform bill . . . No one ever really told us how we are supposed to do that.

To address this gap, Larry and other student leaders approached a social studies teacher, Mrs. Santiago, about implementing an Active Citizenship unit of study in all of her classes, which she agreed to do in order to "build capacity, to build student government back up and make that a central piece in the school for student engagement." Ultimately, student leaders saw school government, and the civic instruction that would help sustain it, as a conduit to address issues with school policies and practices. It was this route that student leaders and Santiago believed would help create a better sense of community throughout the school—a necessary ingredient for addressing some of the larger issues undermining MHS.

STUDENTS USING DEMOCRATIC PROCESSES TO UNDERSTAND SCHOOL PROBLEMS: THE ACTIVE CITIZENSHIP UNIT OF STUDY

The Active Citizenship unit of study was co-taught by Santiago, Larry and a few other student leaders. As mentioned, their goal was to teach students about the constitutional principles that undergird both the school's and the country's democratic system of government, why and how student voice is supposed to operate at MHS, and how to study school problems and use the school government as a conduit for addressing them. Students were to study a particular school program and draw up a proposal to be presented to school government officials.

During the unit of study, Larry and Santiago not only taught the nuts and bolts of how constitutional principles were infused into the school's and the country's governance structure, but also they modeled how researching school problems and actively engaging the school community via democratic processes in order to begin solving them was an application of constitutional concepts. During one lesson, Larry told students, "Without student voice, there is no school. You are just as much a part of the school as anyone. Without your voice, nothing can happen"; then he illustrated how a bill becomes a law. To illustrate the importance of civic participation and how to become agents of change, Larry and other student leaders organized a school-wide walk out in protest of district proposed budget cuts that would eliminate 25 percent of the faculty and staff. The cuts would include the school's only guidance counselor and secretary, radically reduce all funding for after-school activities, and increase class sizes to 35 to 40 students. Less than a week later, nearly the entire school walked out and protested budget cuts in front of the school district's central office. Media coverage of their efforts (student leaders alerted news agencies) and the use of social media networks triggered multiple walk-outs in other schools; and the city saw a rise in after-school protest demonstrations over the next month.

Inspired by the success of their efforts, students formed groups in Santiago's classes during the Active Citizenship unit and began studying other school problems: the causes and effects of the fighting and the peer mediation program and lunch-time conflicts; the allocation of money in the school's budget; the effectiveness of the peer mentorship program; the development of a peer tutoring program; and much more. From these studies emerged program proposals, ideas for new legislation, and immediate changes to some policies and practices. Students also organized multiple bake sales to replace funding that subsidized school trips. I witnessed students cheer in Santiago's classes after several successful fundraisers—a sense of community and ownership over school problems was forming. More students began attending student government planning meetings, and many students expressed interest in running for positions the following year.

By the end of their tenure, Larry and his peers were able to successfully increase student and some faculty engagement with school government, and to build a sense of community throughout the school by getting students to focus on and take ownership over school problems. Student leaders also built the student body's capacity to take on future leadership work and even helped address district budget cuts (some funding was reinstated). If the intention of school reform is to better serve the clients of a school system—namely students—then listening and responding to students and faculty concerns might yield more-informed changes to school policies and practices that can appropriately respond to environmental forces reshaping school life. In addition, this case study indicates that student leadership of the policy creation, implementation and review processes is a promising approach to integrating the concepts of democracy and social justice when researching, discussing and acting on school reform.

Questions to Discuss:

1. Were there exemplars in this case? If so, who were they? Explain.
2. What leadership approaches were developed in the school?
3. Were there any critical incidents in this case? If so, when did they occur and over what issues?
4. When did Madison High School face turbulence? What level of turbulence occurred and why?
5. What were the ethics inculcated in Madison High School's constitution? How were new students introduced to those ethics over time? Discuss.

NOTES

1   All names of people and location have been changed to protect research participants.
2   The National Constitution Center, with its partnering school, has developed a similar model and created a how-to-manual, *We the School.* This manual can be found at http://constitutioncenter.org/learn/educational-resources/lesson-plans/we-the-school

REFERENCES

Arnot, M., & Reay, D. (2004). The social dynamics of classroom learning. In J. Rudduck & D. McIntyre (Eds.) (2007), *Improving learning through consulting pupils.* New York: Routledge.

Brasof, M. (2014). *Student voice in school reform: A case study of Madison High School's youth-adult governance model* (Doctoral dissertation). Available from ProQuest (11670).

Camino, L. (2000). Youth-adult partnerships: Entering new territory in community work and research. *Applied Developmental Science, 4*(1), 11–20. Retrieved from http://www.ecs.org/ecsmain.asp?page=/html/IssueCollapse.asp

Cook-Sather, A. (2002). Authorizing students' perspectives: Toward trust, dialogue, and change in education. *Educational Researcher, 31*(4), 3–14. Retrieved from http://www.jstor.org/stable/3594363

Cook-Sather, A. (2010). Through students' eyes. *Journal of Staff Development, 31*(4), 42–45.

Cook-Sather, A., Cohen, J., & Alter, Z. (2010). Students leading the way toward social justice within and beyond the classroom. *Equity & Excellence in Education, 43*(2), 155–172. doi:10.1080/10665681003719459

Dempster, N. (2006). Leadership for learning: Possible link at the gap state high school. *Leading & Managing: Journal of Australian Council for Educational Administration, 12*(2), 54–63.

Fielding, M. (2001). Students as radical agents of change. *Journal of Educational Change, 2*, 123–141.

Fine, M. (1991). *Framing dropouts: Notes on the politics of an urban high school.* Albany: State University of New York Press.

Johnston, P., & Nicholls, J. (1995). Voices we want to hear and voices we don't. *Theory Into Practice, 34*(2), 94–100.

Kaba, M. (2000/2001). "They listen to me . . . but they don't act on it": Contradictory consciousness and student participation in decision-making. *High School Journal, 82*(2), 21–34.

Mitra, D. (2006). Increasing student voice and moving toward youth leadership. *Prevention Researcher, 13*(1), 7–10.

Mitra, D. (2003). Student voice in school reform: Reframing student-teacher relationships. *McGill Journal of Education, 38*(2), 289–304.

Mitra, D. (2004). The significance of students: Can increasing "student voice" in schools lead to gains in youth development? *Teacher College Record, 106*(4), 651–688.

Pekrul, S., & Levin, B. (2007). Building student voice for school improvement. In D. Thiessen & A. Cook-Sather (Eds.), *International handbook of student experience in elementary and secondary school* (pp. 711–726). Dordrecht: Springer.

Ranjani, R. (2001). *The participation rights of adolescents: A strategic approach.* New York: United Nations Children's Fund, UNICEF Programme Division.

Rudduck, J. (2002). The 2002 SERA lecture: The transformative potential of consulting young people about teaching, learning, and schooling. *Scottish Educational Review, 34*(2), 123–137.

Rudduck, J. (2007). Student voice, student engagement, and school reform. In D. Thiessen & A. Cook-Sather (Eds.), *International handbook of student experience in elementary and secondary school* (pp. 711–726). Dordrecht: Springer.

Rudduck, J., & McIntyre, D. (2007). *Improving learning through consulting pupils.* New York: Routledge.

Stevenson, R. B., & Ellsworth, J. (1991). Dropouts and the silencing of critical voices. In L. Weis & M. Fine (Eds.), *Beyond silenced voices: Class, race, and gender in United States schools.* Albany: State University of New York Press.

Thomson, P., & Holdsworth, R. (2003). Theorizing change in the educational "field": Re-readings of "student participation" projects. *International Journal of Leadership in Education, 6*(4), 371–391.

Wehlage, G. G., Rutter, R. A., Smith, G. A., Lesko, N., & Fernandez, R. R. (1989). *Reducing the risk: Schools as communities of support.* London: Falmer Press.

Zeldin, S. (2004a). Youth as agents of adult and community development: Mapping the processes and outcomes of youth engaged in organizational governance. *Applied Developmental Science, 8*(2), 75–90.

Zeldin, S., Camino, L., & Mook, C. (2005). The adoption of innovation in youth organizations: Creating the conditions for youth-adult partnerships. *Journal of Community Psychology, 33*(1), 121–135. doi:10.1002/jcop.20044

Zeldin, S., McDaniel, A. K., Topitzes, D., & Calvert, M. (2000). *Youth in decision- making: A study on the impacts of youth and adults and organizations.* Madison: Department of Human Development and Family Studies, University of Wisconsin–Madison. Retrieved from http://www.communitybuilders.ro/library/studies/youth-in-decision-making-by-shepherd-zeldin-annette-kusgen-mcdaniel-dimitri-topitzes-matt-calvert/view

Chapter 13

Daanaa Abdullah
Exemplar of Community Leadership
Quisar Abdullah

Daanaa Abdullah was born a Muslim in 1978 in the Caribbean, but he was baptized as a Roman Catholic in 1990. Between 1983 and 1990, he attended various churches and actively participated in various religious and social events, mainly within the various branches of Christianity. After his baptism in 1990, he became a staunch Catholic and continued to practice Catholicism until 1994. In 1995 he converted to Islam. When he converted, he joined one of the more socially active Afro-Caribbean Muslim communities in the Caribbean. The leader of the community he joined often spoke of values such as social responsibility and the need to care for others. Abdullah left the Caribbean in 1997, migrated to the United States, and settled in Philadelphia with his mother and sister. He migrated to Malaysia in 1998 to study at the Islamic university there, and returned to Philadelphia in December 1999. He started at Temple University as an undergraduate student in 2000 and became president of the Muslim Student Association (MSA).

Abdullah reflected on his time as the MSA president, and recalled how he attempted to be democratic. He was in his early twenties, and although he possessed attributes some would term as leadership qualities, he did not receive any formal education or training on how to be an ethical or democratic leader. He remembers that he valued democracy, but he also adopted the more top-down approach to leadership. He would consult or check in with the members of his organization, but he would often make the final decision, even if it was not the most popular, or would sometimes make decisions without consulting his board. He notes now that these types of behavior do not foster positive social interaction or cohesiveness among members. He sees how they are not as "democratic" as he would have liked them to be. He recalls two incidents during his time as president in which he made decisions that were unpopular, but which he felt justified in making.

Abdullah traveled to Puerto Rico during his tenure as president for a student conference. While there, someone had broken into the MSA student office on campus and had stolen some members' belongings. Within a day or so of that incident, another theft took place while the members were praying. The vice president and other members at the time had a suspicion of who had stolen the items, but they did not have clear proof. Nonetheless, they proceeded to ban the person from coming around the organization and reported the person to the Temple University police. Abdullah was informed of this while he was in his hotel in Puerto Rico. He had major issues with this action because he knew and trusted his members, but he also knew that they could not accuse another Muslim of theft without clear proof. Upon his return, he chastised the board for acting on emotion rather than being principled about the process. At the time, he thought he was being fair, in that he knew that he had to uphold the rights and dignity of the person who was merely suspected, since there was no clear proof.

In retrospect, Abdullah realizes that the way he handled the conflict may not have been the best way. In looking back at the incident, he sees that the board members were placing concern and focus on the safety of the other members of the organization, and their possessions. He was focusing on the rights of the individual. Although he has matured, he is still unsure if he would act any differently now. He is of the opinion that a democratic, ethical leader upholds the rights of each individual, even if many others are suspicious of that individual. However, he questions whether or not he is being proud and whether or not he should be humble and let the majority opinion lead his actions. There was no process or facility that mysteriously imbued him with more valuable faculties than other members of his team. He questions whether or not it is a sign of pride that he did not let the majority opinion rule. He was convinced that his opinion held sway, because as a Muslim, he could cite the reason for why someone should not be accused without proof, both from religious text and from the constitution of the United States. He thinks he was being ethical to the individual, but he questions whether or not he was being ethical and just to his team.

This leads to the second incident during Abdullah's tenure as MSA president. He recalls that he was organizing a conference with Muslim students on the East Coast, six months after the attacks of September 11, 2001. The MSA of Temple University was chosen by the national body to host the conference for 2002 on the East Coast. To make it inclusive, the MSA of Temple attempted to allow different universities to lead various standing committees for the conference. In this way, they hoped to make it collaborative. One member of the Temple MSA was chosen to head one of the committees. The university had gone out on holiday break in December. While on break, Abdullah communicated with the MSA at the University of Pennsylvania and realized that they had not been given a committee to coordinate and organize. He then decided, along with one other nonboard member, to have the University of Pennsylvania share the leadership of the committee with the other Temple student chosen to head that committee. The student was not consulted or notified, and only found out indirectly after the fact. A major conflict ensued that threatened to destabilize the conference. Abdullah knew that he had violated basic etiquette, in that he appeared to lack social awareness and understanding of how to make decisions. Additionally, he did not seek meaningful consultation with the person who would be most affected by such a decision. In his mind, he was looking out for the greater benefit—getting all universities on board—but he had missed something even more important, which involved seeking consultation and respecting the rights and sensitivities of others. Additionally, he did not act in the capacity of a transformational leader, but acted in a more authoritarian way. He considered walking away from the position of conference chair because he did not live up to his idea of being a good leader.

At the same time, Abdullah thought that the member should see the bigger picture, which involved getting other universities involved with the planning and organization of the conference. He said that he had a vision for the conference and for the relationship among MSAs in Philadelphia, in which they would share resources and be able to help any Muslim student at any college in Philadelphia. This is the vision he recalls having in his mind. He apologized to the member and attempted to refocus on that. However, he also remembered that he was impatient and questioned the ethics of the member, because the member did not see the big picture. Abdullah sees how his actions were neither democratic nor ethical. He did not consult his team members, and he did not inspire his members to see the vision. He now questions how democratic and ethical he was during that time period. He states that he is not sure if one ethical characteristic supersedes another characteristic at any point throughout the process. If it is possible to suppress one characteristic in favor of another at a certain point, does that raise questions about the leader's ethical stance? He is wrestling with whether or not ethics are absolute or malleable depending on the needs of the moment. If ethics are malleable, then it needs to be clear as to under what conditions ethics are malleable and who is then to make that decision or evaluation.

In looking at both conflicts, although Abdullah had questions about his overall actions, I attempted to evaluate how his actions and decision making process fit with the harmony model of conflict resolution—and if Abdullah could have made those decisions if he did not place a value on ethics.

In the first example, he tried to resolve the issue by finding a common value that all the members possessed. He knew that all members valued the religious texts, so he attempted to show how his opinion was validated by the text. However, in looking at this critically, that is a tactic that many use to justify their personal stance and opinions on certain topics. The ability to validate an opinion based on a collectively espoused value does not necessarily make the action any more ethical. The harmony model would say that, to minimize a conflict, there must be a reference to a collective value. Although Abdullah called on this collective value, it does not make him democratic. However, some would argue that he was ethical in the decision and the process he used to demonstrate why that action was the best course of action. In the second conflict, Abdullah utilized a socially derived ethic of community and collaboration to justify why he made the decision he made. However, this does not absolve him of the error of making that decision without proper consultation. He demonstrated steadfastness and resilience, but he did not show a certain degree of humility or tact. He was able to minimize the conflict using ideas from the harmony model, but he did not demonstrate a clear democratic orientation in the methods he used to resolve the conflicts.

Questions to Discuss:

1. Who was the exemplar in this case? Would you call him a transformative leader? Why or why not?
2. What leadership style did he exhibit? Describe.
3. What were the critical incidents in this case? How did the leader deal with them and what did he do in retrospect?
4. What was the turbulence level in both of these cases? How did the leader increase or decrease the levels?
5. What kinds of ethics did this leader turn to? Did he focus on the ethics of justice, critique, care, profession and/or community? Discuss.

ETHICAL DECISION-MAKING[1]

New DEEL Vision for Educational Leaders	Behavior of Conventional School Leaders
4. Operates from a deep understanding of ethical decision-making in the context of a dynamic, inclusive, democratic vision.	Operates largely from perspective of the ethic of justice wherein obedience to authority and current regulations is largely unquestioned despite one's own misgivings.

In Part IV, the focus is on ethical decision-making. As a New DEEL educational leader, it is important to ask two major questions: How do we know we are facing an ethical decision? And how do we make an ethical decision? Turning to the first question, we need to understand paradoxes or contradictory messages.

In his book *Reflections on the Moral and Spiritual Crisis in Education* (2004), David Purpel puts forth a number of paradoxes. One of these paradoxes is Individuality versus Community. Purpel speaks of individuality in regards to the embedded values in American society of the "Rugged Individual," the Puritan work ethic, and the Frontier Thesis. There are positive aspects of this concept, because it has created a country of people who are keen to succeed, to make themselves better and better—and in so doing, it is hoped that this will make society better and better. However, there are negative aspects of this credo: greed and narcissism are offshoots of these beliefs. There also can be much loneliness, often related to small families, divorce, and single parents.

On the other hand, this society has had at its heart a focus on community. This can be seen in the words of the Declaration of Independence, the

Constitution, and the Gettysburg Address (all discussed during inaugural celebrations). All these documents deal with aspects of nationhood, peoplehood, union, common purpose, and common destiny. We celebrate bonding rituals—July 4th, Mother's and Father's Days, and graduation. Our politicians try to reach out to the community and greater society. They use town meetings, public debates, and all kinds of grassroots techniques to be elected. They reach into local society and campaign on the values of a positive community.

In our schools, we often give mixed messages and create paradoxes inadvertently. On the one hand, public schools stress the importance of individual achievement with an emphasis on normative grading, on standardized high-stakes tests, on tracking of students by abilities, on special education individualized education programs (IEPs), and on gifted and talented programs.

On the other hand, in sports programs, there is talk of a community of individuals making up a team and everyone helping each other. Community also can be seen in the form of parents groups associated with the schools, the choral society, the school spirit, and school traditions. Alumni/ ae support also helps in creating a sense of community.

Hopefully, in this example of Individuality versus Community, the paradox is now clearly visible. These contradictions can be found not only in schools, but also in other institutions and even in our homes. They can be difficult and challenging for students to understand. Adults need to keep paradoxes in mind when making ethical decisions.

The second major question, raised at the beginning of this introduction, was: How do we make an ethical decision? In response to this query, there are a number of ethical decision-making models in the educational leadership literature (e.g., Branson, 2014; Dantley, 2005; Starratt. 1994; Tuana, 2014). One of those models is called the Multiple Ethical Paradigms (MEP) model (Shapiro & Gross, 2013; Shapiro & Stefkovich, 2011). This is the model that we will focus on in Part IV for assistance in making ethical educational decisions. MEP provides four perspectives or paradigms. It encompasses the ethics of justice, critique, care, and the profession.

The ethic of justice focuses on laws, rights, and policies, and is part of a liberal democratic tradition that, according to Delgado (1995), "is characterized by incrementalism, faith in the legal system, and hope for progress" (p. 1). Starratt (1994) described the ethic of justice as emanating from two schools of thought: one originating in the 17th century including the work of Hobbes, Kant, and more contemporary scholars such as Rawls and Kohlberg; the other rooted in the works of philosophers such as Aristotle, Rousseau, Hegel, Marx, and Dewey. The former school sees the individual as central and social relationships as a type of a social contract where the individual, using human reason, gives up some rights for the good of the whole or for social justice (Starratt, 1994, p. 49). The latter school tends to see society as central rather than the individual, and it seeks to teach individuals how to behave throughout their life within communities. In this tradition, justice emerges from "communal understandings" (Starratt, 1994, p. 50). Educators and ethicists from the ethic of justice (e.g., Beauchamp & Childress, 1984; Strike, Haller, & Soltis, 2005) have profoundly impacted approaches to education and educational leadership. This ethic includes concepts such as fairness, equality, and freedom. Questions to consider under this paradigm are: Is there a law, right, or policy appropriate for this situation? Why is this ethic the correct one? If so, how should it be implemented?

A number of writers and activists (e.g., Apple, 2003; Bakhtin, 1981; Freire, 1970; Giroux, 2006; Greene, 1988) are not convinced by the analytic and rational approach of the justice paradigm; they turn to the ethic of critique. They raise difficult questions by critiquing both the laws themselves and the process used to determine if the laws are just. This ethic asks us to redefine and challenge concepts. It deals with power, privilege, and social justice. This ethic is based on critical theory that focuses on an analysis of social class and its inequities. Along with critical theory, the ethic of critique is also frequently linked to critical pedagogy. Scholars, practicing this approach, are also activists who believe discourse should be a beginning that leads to some kind of action—preferably political. For example, Shapiro and Purpel (2005) emphasize empowering people through the discussion of options. Such a dialogue hopefully would provide what Giroux and Aronowitz (1985) call a "language of possibility" that might enable educational institutions to avoid reproducing the "isms" in society (i.e., classism, racism, sexism, heterosexism) and instead provide opportunities for all to grow, learn, and achieve. This ethic asks educators to deal with the hard questions regarding social class, race, gender, and other areas of difference, such as: Who makes the laws, rules, or policies? Who benefits from them? Who has the power? Who is silenced?

Some feminist scholars (e.g., Beck, 1994; Belenky, Clinchy, Goldberger, & Tarule, 1986; Gilligan, 1982; Marshall & Oliva, 2006; Noddings, 2003) have challenged the dominant, and generally more patriarchal, ethic of justice by turning to the ethic of care for moral decision-making. Similar to critical theorists, these feminist scholars emphasize social responsibility and social justice as pivotal concepts related to the ethic of care. While the ethic of care has been associated with feminists, men and women alike attest to its importance and relevancy. Male ethicists and educators such as John Stuart Mills, David Hume, and Jeremy Bentham, as well as the more contemporary Blackburn (2001), Buber (1965), and Sergiovanni (2009), to name but a few, have expressed high regard for this paradigm. This ethic requests individuals to consider the consequences of their decisions and actions.

It deals with loyalty, trust, and empowerment. It asks them to consider questions such as: Who will benefit from what I decide? Who will be hurt by my actions? What are the long-term effects of my decision? If I am helped by someone today, how can I give back to society in the future?

In recent years, there has been a resurgence of interest in professional ethics for educational leaders. A number of writers in educational administration (e.g., Beck & Murphy, 1994; Begley & Johansson, 2003; Duke & Grogan, 1997; and Starratt, 2004) believe it is important to provide prospective administrators with some training in ethics. This ethic contains one's personal and professional codes and professional organizations' codes of ethics, including the National Policy Board's ISLLC's Standards (NPBEA, 2008) and state educational standards. Above all, at the heart of the ethic of the profession, Shapiro and Stefkovich have placed the *Best Interests of the Student.* This concept is especially important, because in this era it is hard not to place the budget at the center of the decision-making process.

Unfortunately, the ethic of the profession may contain clashes. For example, there may be clashes between an individual's personal and professional code of ethics. There may be conflicts within professional codes. There may be clashes between professional codes among educational leaders. Finally, there could be clashes between a leader's personal and professional code of ethics, and customs and practices set forth by the local community.

Although the MEP model contains the ethic of the community, Furman (2004; Furman-Brown, 2002), a professor from Washington State University, thinks of it as freestanding and not part of a more complicated model. She describes the ethic of community as an ongoing process, leading to consensus, in making an ethical decision.

The exemplars in Part IV all have to face paradoxes or inconsistencies and have to make challenging ethical decisions. Most tend to use multiple ethical perspectives in making their decisions. In the first chapter, written by Lynne Blair, Darrell Scott made an ethical decision to try to transform schools from being sites of bullying and violence to institutions that value kindness and compassion. Following in the footsteps of his daughter, Rachel, who was killed at Columbine High School in 1999, he asks students to become caring individuals who will not allow hatred and fear to dominate their culture. Darrell Scott's vision values diversity and attempts to give all students a voice to fight injustices. Rachel's Challenge is being spread through the Friends of Rachel Clubs that have been established in many schools throughout the U.S. and beyond.

The next chapter, developed by Val Storey, focuses on Dr. Cynthia Gomez, a school administrator. When a shooting occurred in the community involving students from her school, Dr. Gomez went to the hospital and helped the victim's family. However, she did not take sides, but instead waited to find out what had actually occurred. Her wise ethical decision-making regarding this very disturbing incident enabled her to act as a true leader who exhibited an inclusive, thoughtful, and balanced approach in seeking to help both the victim and the accused.

Patricia A. L. Ehrensal's chapter highlights Elsa Prendergast, a first-year principal of an elementary school that was in terrible shape in a poverty-stricken community. Two years after she arrived, Ms. Prendergast transformed the school into a warm, welcoming, and safe place. She accomplished this positive change through distributive leadership and a very inclusive attitude. She worked closely not only with the teachers, but also with the parents. In particular, this case raises the question: Can a school thrive once a transformative leader has left?

Peter Brigg writes about an elementary school principal who finds out about a district plan to start incentive pay for student performance on state tests. Opposed to the plan, this principal decided to use ethical reasoning, considered deliberations, fact finding, and quiet strength in response. It is not easy or always safe to take this kind of stand against forthcoming district policy, but this chapter shows a compelling way this might be accomplished.

NOTE

1 Some of the material for the introduction to this part has been borrowed from Chapter 2 of Shapiro and Stefkovich (2011), and Chapter 2 of Shapiro and Gross (2013).

REFERENCES

Apple, M. W. (2003). *The state and the politics of knowledge.* New York: RoutledgeFalmer.

Bakhtin, M. (1981). *The dialogic imagination.* Austin: University of Texas Press.

Beauchamp, T. L., & Childress, J. F. (1984). Morality, ethics and ethical theories. In P. Sola (Ed.), *Ethics, education, and administrative decisions: A book of readings* (pp. 39–67). New York: Peter Lang.

Beck, L. G. (1994). *Reclaiming educational administration as a caring profession.* New York: Teachers College Press.

Beck, L. G., & Murphy, J. (1994). *Ethics in educational leadership programs: An expanding role.* Thousand Oaks, CA: Corwin Press.

Begley, P. T., & Johansson, O. (Eds.). (2003). *The ethical dimensions of school leadership.* Boston: Kluwer Academic.

Belenky, M. F., Clinchy, B. M., Goldberger, N. R., & Tarule, J. M. (1986). *Women's ways of knowing.* New York: Basic Books.

Blackburn, S. (2001). *Being good: A short introduction to ethics.* Oxford: Oxford University Press.

Branson, C. M. (2014). "Maintaining moral integrity." In C. M. Branson & S. J. Gross (Eds.), *Handbook of ethical educational leadership* (pp. 263–281). New York: Routledge.

Buber, M. (1965). Education. In M. Buber (Ed.), *Between man and man* (pp. 83–103). New York: Macmillan.

Dantley, M.E. (2005). Moral leadership: Shifting the management paradigm. In F.W. English (Ed.), *The Sage handbook of educational leadership: Advances in theory, research, and practice*, pp. 36–46. Thousand Oaks, CA: Sage.

Delgado, R. (1995). *Critical race theory: The cutting edge.* Philadelphia, PA: Temple University Press.

Duke, D., & Grogan, M. (1997). The moral and ethical dimensions of leadership. In L. G. Beck, J. Murphy, & Associates (Eds.), *Ethics in educational leadership programs: emerging models* (pp. 141–160). Columbia, MO: University Council for Educational Administration.

Freire, P. (1970). *Pedagogy of the oppressed* (M.B. Ramos, trans.). New York: Continuum.

Furman, G.C. (2004). The ethic of community. *Journal of Educational Administration, 42,* 215–235.

Furman-Brown, G. (Ed.). (2002). *School as community: From promise to practice.* Albany: State University of New York Press.

Gilligan, C. (1982). *In a different voice.* Cambridge, MA: Harvard University Press.

Giroux, H. A. (2006). *America on the edge: Henry Giroux on politics, education and culture.* New York: Palgrave MacMillan.

Giroux, H.A., & Aronowitz, S. (1985). *Education under siege.* South Hadley, MA: Bergin & Garvey.

Greene, M. (1988). *The dialectic of freedom.* New York: Teachers College Press.

Marshall, C., & Oliva, M. (2006). *Leadership for social justice: Making revolutions in education.* Boston, MA: Allyn & Bacon.

National Policy Board for Educational Administration (NPBEA). (2008). Educational leadership policy standards: ISLLC 2008, pp. 1–5. Washington, DC: Council of Chief State School Officers. Retrieved January 3, 2010, from http://www.ccsso.org/content/pdfs/elps_isllc2008.pdf

Noddings, N. (2003). *Caring: A feminine approach to ethics and moral education* (2nd ed.). Berkeley: University of California Press.

Sergiovanni, T. J. (2009). *The principalship: A reflective practice perspective* (6th ed.). Boston: Allen & Bacon.

Shapiro, H.S., & Purpel, D.E. (Eds.). (2005). *Social issues in American education: Democracy and meaning in a globalized world* (3rd ed.). Mahwah, NJ: Lawrence Erlbaum Associates.

Shapiro, J. P., & Gross, S. J. (2013). *Ethical Educational leadership in turbulent times: (Re)solving moral dilemmas* (2nd ed.). New York: Routledge.

Shapiro, J.P., & Stefkovich, J.A. (2011). *Ethical leadership and decision making in education: Applying theoretical perspectives to complex dilemmas* (3rd ed.). New York: Routledge.

Starratt, R.J. (1994). *Building an ethical school.* London: Falmer Press.

Starratt, R.J. (2004). *Ethical leadership.* San Francisco, CA: Jossey-Bass.

Strike, K.A., Haller, E.J., & Soltis, J.F. (2005). *The ethics of school administration* (3rd ed.). New York: Teachers College Press.

Tuana, N. (2014). An ethical leadership developmental framework. In C. M. Branson & S. J. Gross (Eds.), *Handbook of ethical educational leadership* (pp. 153–175). New York: Routledge.

Chapter 14

Rachel's Challenge
A Caring Connection

Lynne Blair

On April 20, 1999, gunshots and violence permeated throughout Columbine High School in Littleton, Colorado. Eric Harris and Dylan Klebold entered the school that morning with ninety-five explosive devises in total; they had enough firepower to destroy their entire school and potentially take the lives of hundreds of students and teachers. What was the result of their hatred and diabolical aggression? The lives of twelve students and one teacher were lost in the name of school violence. It was a historical day in our nation's history because it etched into our minds the reality of a school massacre, and it will forever be a day of rage, grief, and suffering for those left to face the confusion and devastation surrounding the lives lost. It is nearly impossible to fathom how families, friends, the school, and the larger community could move forward from this monumental event.

Eric Harris, one of the two shooters, said, "We need to . . . kick start a revolution. We need to get a chain reaction going here." His actions indeed created a revolution of fear; a revolution of awareness of the repercussions of bullying and social exclusion and isolation; a revolution of accountability for all the violence that adolescents are exposed to through video games, movies, and music; and a revolution of tremendous pain and grief. The chain reaction that Eric and Dylan created that day began from a place of anger and hurt, and the aftermath has proven to bring continued hurt and pain to the families and friends of the victims, as well as the community at large. Their negative chain reaction outlived them and will forever burden the survivors who witnessed such inconceivable violence, the victims' loved ones, and the larger community that believed devastation of this caliber could never find its way into their utopian existence. Dylan's and Eric's first victim was Rachel Scott. Rachel and Eric, ironically, shared a similar vision—a faith in the power of a chain reaction. In an essay for her English class, Rachel wrote, "I have this theory that if one person can go out of their way to show compassion, then it will start a chain reaction of the same." Rachel's chain reaction differed from Eric's in that she believed in spreading forth compassion, kindness, and acceptance. She believed in a chain reaction of love. Rachel befriended the students in her school who were marginalized; she spread compassion and believed in random acts of kindness directed toward strangers, she believed in the good nature of humanity, she dared to dream and was empowered by her vision of a kinder world, and she was relentless in her pursuit to challenge the status quo of selfishness, bullying, exclusion, and isolation.

After Rachel's death, some of her peers and people outside of her school came forward with stories of how Rachel had impacted their lives. She helped students feel stronger and more accepted, she gave away material things to those who were in need, she reached out to those who were struggling and instilled in them a will to live at times, she provided people with a nonjudgmental perspective, and she believed in a world where love and kindness could triumph and prevail. Like Eric's chain reaction, Rachel's chain reaction has continued beyond the length of her lifetime. And that is in no small part due to the efforts of one man—Darrell Scott.

After the horrific loss of his daughter, Darrell Scott was faced with a level of grief that is incomprehensible to most of us. Not only was Rachel's life cut unfairly short, but her life was sacrificed and lost in the face of such devastating violence. Darrell's daring choice to forgive Eric and Dylan, and to use their choice for violence as a catalyst to promote a democratic and dynamic vision in schools across the world through his creation of the Rachel's Challenge program, is absolutely epic and heroic. He defines, for me, what it takes to be an educational leader. He focuses on promoting a humanistic perspective and developing adolescents' character.

After Rachel's death, Darrell was faced with a critical incident in his own life—one that could potentially break who he was as a person. Rather than let the violence of Columbine destroy him, Darrell used the violence to effect serious change in the lives of countless people, and that change is due to a chain reaction of goodness started with his daughter's value system. Rachel's Challenge was developed by Darrell to inspire students to make changes in their lives and in their schools by treating others with kindness and compassion, in an effort to promote Rachel's legacy. It is a comprehensive approach to character education with two components: an assembly program delivered to an entire school community (and parents), and the teaching of a character education curriculum to a selected group of student leaders. These student leaders are trained to start a Rachel's Challenge club within their school to continue the development and promotion of the values of the Rachel's Challenge program. The assembly program speakers are either family members of Rachel Scott, victims of the tragedy who were fortunate enough to survive the massacre, family members of victims of the tragedy who lost their lives, or other individuals chosen by and trained by Darrell Scott. The general assembly for the high school students involves showing a video of the Columbine tragedy, and a message from Rachel Scott, delivered by the speaker, about hope and the deliverance of a challenge to students to make a positive difference in their schools.

Ultimately, Darrell asks the students to become their own educational leaders within their schools and to change the environment. It is a powerful message for students, designed to touch their hearts and encourage them to care about one another. Following the all-school assembly program, a selected group of student leaders attend a training workshop with the assembly facilitator. The curriculum used for the training of the student leaders focuses on looking for the best in others, dreaming and setting goals, choosing positive influences, demonstrating acts of kindness, and starting a chain reaction of positive, kind actions. The students are trained for future work within the school through the development of a Rachel's Challenge club to create a culture of kindness and compassion; the leaders are encouraged to critically analyze organizational structures, develop positive student interactions and relationships, appreciate diversity, make kindness and compassion the norm, and create a more democratic culture within their schools. Students are trained to be leaders and implement projects throughout the school year to reinforce the messages of the program. Darrell Scott wanted to create a program with the following basic tenet:

> The most discouraging symptom of American life today has been the growth in the last ten years of social intolerance. We need the schools to bring about recognition of the problems . . . things which the American people have got to work out together in a spirit of unity and cooperation . . . one act of kindness and compassion can start a chain reaction and, with nurturing, transform the culture in schools.
>
> (Hollingshead, Crump, Eddy, & Rowe, 2009, p. 112)

The program is established to transform the culture of a school by valuing diversity, giving all students a voice, making kindness and compassion the norm, reflecting on social injustices within the school, focusing on personal growth and development, valuing service to the school and the larger community, recognizing one's own power of influence, setting personal goals, removing prejudice and bias, and promoting a positive sense of community (Hollingshead et al., 2009). Darrell's extraordinary choice to create the Rachel's Challenge program demonstrates the power of forgiveness, the need for individuals to have a level of resilience to foster healthy responses to adversity, and the everlasting potential of positive chain reactions.

Questions to Discuss:

1. Would you think of both Rachel and her father, Darrell Scott, as exemplars? If so, why would they be thought of in this way? Discuss.
2. What was the critical incident in this case? Provide some details.
3. What leadership style did Rachel use? What leadership style did Darrell Scott exhibit?
4. What kind of ethical decision-making did Darrell Scott turn to in developing Rachel's Challenge? Did he focus on the ethic of justice, critique, care, and/or the profession? Explain.
5. Did Darrell Scott do anything to manage the turbulence level in Columbine High School and in other schools in the U.S.? Discuss.

REFERENCE

Hollingshead, B., Crump, C., Eddy, R., & Rowe, D. (2009). Rachel's challenge: A moral compass for character education. *Kappa Delta Pi Record, 45*(3), 111–115.

Chapter 15

Reclaiming School Reform From Duty to Care

Valerie A. Storey

The challenges facing present-day school leaders, both in the urban and rural community arenas, have never been more complex, as they must

> grapple with federal and state legislative requirements, accountability man-dates, teacher performance incentives, changing student demographics, and data driven decision making. They must also meet requests from district office, the school board and the community they serve for greater transpar-ency and accountability.
>
> (Storey, 2010, p. 59)

This increasing complexity of school leadership has been evidenced by the number of school leaders confessing to finding their role and responsibili-ties to be overwhelming at times as they struggle with a host of strategic and operational areas. While recognizing there are no quick fixes, every aspir-ing school leader aims to lead a school of excellence that effectively raises student achievement in an increasingly diverse cultural environment: "The expectation is that a school leader will absorb the culture of the school and be able to avoid real problems that are often the result of 'novice' or 'rookie' decision making" (Storey, 2010, p. 60).

The critical incident below, written from Dr. Cynthia Gomez's viewpoint, describes the unfolding events of one evening that occurred in the vicinity of a magnet middle school situated in a large school district in the south-eastern United States (V.A. Storey, personal communication, March 2014). The school serves approximately 1,200 students in grades 6–8:

> The day began just like any other normal fall day. I arrived at work at approxi-mately 6:30am and for the next twelve hours worked closely with teachers,

students and their parents. I then moved to my office where I began to work through the administrative tasks that had accumulated on my desk. The next thing I knew was that the sky outside my window was dark and that I was feeling hungry. Around 9:00pm I received a call on my work cell phone from a number I did not recognize. Due to the lateness of the hour and the fact that I was alone on the campus I did not respond. My personal cell phone then rang and it was from a number that I did recognize. It was the number of my immediate supervisor, who is the principal of my campus. I immediately answered the call.

Sadly, I learned that there had been a shooting incident in the local community and there were scant details available. It seemed that both of the young people involved were currently enrolled at our school. My principal had been informed that the incident had happened in a home rather than on the street. My first thought was that this might be a gang related incident which could result in serious repercussions amongst the school community, but my principal was of the view that this was an isolated incident. I was extremely concerned about both students' health at this point: for the student that had been shot, but also for the mental well-being of the alleged aggressor. I spoke with my principal for a few more minutes but as he had no additional information to share, we said our goodnights and that we would meet first thing in the morning to further discuss the incident. As soon as I put the phone down my thoughts turned to my students and their families.

As an educational leader some decisions we make are well thought-out, deliberated at length and critically assessed before being acted upon. In this circumstance, as an educational leader, no contemplation was needed. I was there to help the students succeed; to congratulate them on their successes, but also to console and support them during difficult times. I immediately decided to go to the store to purchase a teddy bear, balloons, card, and some flowers for the victim who I understood had been taken by emergency services to the local hospital.

By the time I arrived at the hospital it was very late and yet not surprisingly there was a lot of activity going on inside and outside the building. I discovered that the student who was allegedly the guilty party had left the area and the police were looking for him.

There were several groups of visibly distraught people in various areas of the hospital. The first group I approached turned out to be family members of the victim. I was introduced to the victim's grandmother who was visibly upset and was requesting a cup of coffee from a gentleman that I think was her son, the student's uncle. The grandmother was told that there was no coffee at the location and the cafeteria was closed. The machine they were trying to get it from was broken.

As an educational leader, I believe that my responsibilities go above and beyond the classroom and the students themselves, and that my commitment extends to their families and the overall community. A good leader knows that the family and community will support your efforts, and in turn that they need your support as well. As such it was an easy decision to offer to help and calm the situation by volunteering to drive down the road to an off-site restaurant to purchase the grandmother a cup of coffee.

I did so and returned back to the hospital with the coffee and went on to give it to grandmother and to let her know that I was there both professionally and personally and if there were anything that I could do to assist or support the family then would they please let me know. Either my company or the coffee calmed her down. Having ensured that she was safe for the moment I went to speak with what I believe were additional family members, aunts and cousins, who were also waiting around for news.

The hospital stated that they were not allowing visitors in at that point but the cousins gave me an update in regards to the victim's condition. Her prognosis was good, her condition had stabilized, and she was no longer in a critical condition.

I was ecstatic to hear that she was doing well, and informed the parents that I was delighted by the news. I left the items that I had brought, and signed the card. I explained in the card that if there was anything further I could do to help then they should not hesitate to contact me. I also stated that my colleagues and I were here for her, we care for her, we love her, and wanted her to know that our thoughts and prayers were with her and the family. I also signed the names of my other administrators. Although I did not get their approval I do believe that they would not have minded that I wanted to share their names, as I firmly believe that had they received the late night phone call they would also have journeyed immediately to the hospital.

I continued to support the family as they negotiated the sterile and rather alienating hospital environment. At midnight I left the hospital.

I later learned that the shooting was an accident and that it did happen at the home. I also offered condolences to the young man's family that was probably going through a lot emotionally at this time and also offered the victim's parents some information about counseling and how to get through things like this and also whatever I could offer them in the future in relation to this. Both families that I spoke to were very grateful that I was there and very appreciative of the fact.

While everything happened so quickly, and I did take immediate action, looking back I can see value in not rushing to judgment too hastily. To my fellow educational leaders, I can say that our role in these situations is not to take sides but to help console all affected parties.

The next morning we had an emergency school meeting in regards to the process so that our students on our campus could feel consoled and safe and also have discussion about gun safety and about the possible way to deal with your emotions when things of this magnitude occur. Our grief counselors were on campus for the week and ready for our students in the multi-purpose room as well as the media center with tissues, supplies, and phones so that we could make sure that our students were taken care of in a manner that is conducive for each of them individually.

When I returned to campus the following week I received the students' mailing information and mailed home cards to the victim and the accused families. I wanted to let them know that we are still here for them and if there is anything that we can do to please let us know, and that we are certainly still thinking about them.

Note: In the year after the December 2012 Newtown, Connecticut, school massacre, 194 children ages 12 and under were shot to death in the U.S. At least 52 of those deaths involved a child handling an unsecured gun, and 127 of the children died in their own homes. The problem was worse during that year in the South, which saw at least 92 child gun deaths, followed by the Midwest (44), the West (38), and the East (20) (Follman, 2013).

Questions to Discuss:

1. Was Dr. Gomez an exemplar who exhibited a deep understanding of ethical decision making? If so, explain. If not, explain why not.
2. Did Dr. Gomez display a particular kind of leadership style? If so, what was it?
3. What was the critical incident in this case? Provide some details.
4. What ethical lens or lenses did Dr. Gomez turn to in order to make her decisions in this case? Discuss the different lenses that she used or did not use.
5. Initially, what was the turbulence level in this story? Did Dr. Gomez have a positive or negative impact regarding this situation? Explain.

REFERENCES

Follman, M. (2013). *Newtown one year after.* Retrieved from http://www.motherjones.com/special-reports/2013/12/newtown-shooting-one-year-later
Storey, V. A. (2010). *New DEEL: An ethical framework for addressing common issues in Florida schools.* Palm Beach, FL: JAPSS Press.

Chapter 16

The Limits of a Single Candle

Patricia A. L. Ehrensal

It is better to light a candle than curse the darkness.[1]

It had to be one of the gloomiest school buildings I have ever been in. The walls were a dark brown color, doubtlessly chosen for its durability rather than aesthetics. There were no student art works or projects decorating the hallway—odd, I thought, for an elementary school. As my companion and I walked to the library, I remarked that I wouldn't send my cat there for school. It was early September in what I later learned to be Elsa Prendergast's first year as principal of Hunsford Elementary School.[2]

Two years later, when I attended another meeting there, I found the school transformed. The walls had been painted a bright cream color and were covered with projects and art. One of the closets had been taken over by the students in the 5th-grade social studies and art classes, who were in the process of converting it into a burial chamber in a pyramid, complete with art and artifacts. The burial chamber was the feature project for the upcoming Art & Music Night, which would exhibit the children's learning and skills to the parents and community members who would be attending.

The demographics of the school had not changed. The children still came from the poorest neighborhoods in the school district, which included the local homeless shelter, and the school had the most children in both Title I and the free and reduced lunch program. Yet, the joy of learning was palpable as I walked to the library. Unlike my last experience, PTA moms were there to serve the refreshments they had made for those attending the meeting, and the children had made a banner welcoming the attendees to their school. Elsa Prendergast personally greeted each attendee. After the meeting,

I reintroduced myself to Ms. Prendergast and asked her if I could come one day soon to visit the school when the children were there. She said I was welcome at any time, and an appointment was made for the following week.

When I arrived at the school on the appointed day, Elsa and two 5th-grade boys who were members of the *Banner Wagon* greeted me at the door. The boys took me on a tour of the school, during which they demonstrated a good deal of knowledge about the school, teachers, staff and students. During the tour and in the classroom I observed, the children's excitement and love of learning was unmistakable. When I returned to her office, I remarked to Elsa about the extraordinary changes at Hunsford. While these changes were multifaceted, here I will focus on the three that demonstrate characteristics of democratic ethical educational leadership: distributed leadership, reaching out to the community and developing a PTA, and instituting the *Banner Wagon*.

DISTRIBUTIVE LEADERSHIP

Elsa, as principal, explained her vision of a school community to the faculty, in which she saw herself as a "first among equals." That is, her job was to facilitate the work of the school; however, the teachers were equal partners. Elsa saw her role as coordinating the efforts of the faculty (Mintzberg, 1979); seeking resources and liaising with Central Office, particularly the superintendent (Pfeffer & Salancik, 1978); and advocating for the school (Mintzberg, 1983). The efforts for improving teaching and learning, however, were to be determined by the teachers. The first task they agreed to undertake was decorating the entry hall. Elsa was able to obtain the paint supplies from the school district, and the teachers volunteered to do the painting. However, there were no funds available for bulletin boards. Elsa did discover that Hunsford had $250 collected in memory of a much-loved custodian who had died a year earlier. Elsa proposed that these funds be used to purchase the bulletin boards, and the teachers agreed. A plaque was also placed over the bulletin boards stating that they were purchased in memory of the custodian. The entire staff and many of the parents agreed that he would have appreciated this gesture. With its bright cream paint and the children's artwork on the new bulletin boards, the entry way was now warm and welcoming.

REACHING OUT TO THE COMMUNITY AND
ESTABLISHING A PTA

One of the charges Elsa was given by the Superintendent was to establish a PTA at Hunsford. During the faculty meeting discussion of the upcoming

Open House, Elsa was informed that they didn't plan any special program, and that the teachers mostly stayed in their classrooms. When she asked why, the teachers told her that very few people come to Open House, and the general consensus was because "these people" don't care about their kids. Elsa approached parents and asked why they didn't come to Open House. The parents told her that the neighborhood wasn't safe after dark, so they didn't want to be out at night. Through these discussions, Elsa learned that parents could come at lunchtime and right after school. She received permission from the Superintendent to allow parents to come at lunchtime and have other programs start right after school. For the first afterschool Open House, the custodian only set up two rows of chairs, claiming that it was more than enough. However, he and the Superintendent had to scramble to set up many extra rows as the parents flowed in. By simply asking for the parents' input and acknowledging the legitimacy of the community (Furhman, 2004), Hunsford had an active PTA within two years and one of the district's highest attendance rates at Open House and Art & Music Night. The teachers valued the parents, and the school became more welcoming to the community.

ESTABLISHING THE *BANNER WAGON*

Transient students were a significant issue at Hunsford. Some of the children lived in the homeless shelter, and others moved in and out of the neighborhood and the school for economic reasons. Although a student might be there only a short time, Elsa and the teachers understood that these children had a right to an education; but in order to learn, the students had to feel they were part of the school community. To ensure this, the Hunsford *Banner Wagon* was established. Students from the 5th-grade class took on leadership roles to ensure that all new students were welcomed and incorporated into the school community as quickly as possible. They helped children find their classroom, and they made sure children did not eat lunch alone and were included in playground games.

DEMOCRATIC ETHICAL EDUCATIONAL LEADERSHIP

Elsa's leadership was grounded in democratic and ethical principles. Her actions acknowledged *rights*, accepted *responsibility*, and demonstrated *respect*, consistent with the ethic of justice (Shapiro & Stefkovich, 2011; Starratt, 2012; Stefkovich, 2006). Through her leadership, Elsa fostered the ethic of justice among the teachers and staff at Hunsford as they developed a commitment to the students' *right* to education regardless of their race, socio-economic status, or current situation. They acknowledged their *responsibility* to foster a school community where the children would feel valued and accepted. Finally, the teachers developed a sense of self-respect as professionals, as well as a growing *respect* for the members of the community, and an understanding that their precarious situation was not a measure of their worth; and consequently, they acknowledged the importance of their voice and the need to seek common ground. Elsa's commitment to distributive leadership fostered a more collaborative and democratic approach to decision-making processes. Additionally, these democratic processes allowed for "reframing and constructing knowledge for mutual concern and fostering collaborative community processes committed to fairness" (Gerstl-Pepin & Aiken, 2009, p. 419).

THE LIMITS OF A SINGLE CANDLE

Elsa eventually left Hunsford for a Central Office position in another school district; however, she maintained a relationship with several of the teachers. Both Elsa and the teachers were dismayed at how quickly life at Hunsford reverted to its former state. This was not the result of a *leadership of one* masquerading as democratic leadership (Woods, 2009). Rather, I argue that it was the result of the larger structure. Hunsford is a school embedded in a school district organizational culture, which in turn is embedded in a state and national education culture. While Elsa's democratic and ethical leadership did change the practices and surface culture of Hunsford (Schein, 2010), the deep organizational culture of the district (Martin, 1992), with all of its deep-rooted inequities, was unaltered. Consequently, the changes in Hunsford couldn't be sustained after Elsa left. By lighting a single candle at Hunsford, Elsa certainly shined light on the possibilities. However, for democratic ethical leadership to take hold, the larger cultural structure of education must be addressed. Otherwise educational leaders will continue to stumble around in the semi-darkness of inequity and inequality.

Questions to Discuss:

1. Who was the exemplar in this case, and what made her so outstanding? Describe.
2. What were the major issues that the exemplar faced?
3. Did Elsa Prendergast exhibit an inclusive and democratic vision? Explain.
4. How turbulent was Elsa's school when she became its leader? What did she do to lower the turbulence level?

5. What kinds of ethics did this leader use for ethical decision-making? Did she turn to the ethics of justice, critique, care, and/or the profession? Discuss.

NOTES

1   An old Chinese proverb used by Adlai Stevenson when describing Eleanor Roosevelt in a 1962 *New York Times* article (Simpson & Speake, 2008).
2   Both Elsa Prendergast and Hunsford Elementary School are pseudonyms.

REFERENCES

Furman, G. C. (2004). The ethic of community. *Journal of Educational Administration, 42*(2), 215–235.

Gerstl-Pepin, C., & Aiken, J. (2009). Democratic school leaders: Defining ethical leadership in a standardized context. *Journal of School Leadership, 19*(4), 406–444.

Martin, J. (1992). *Culture in organizations: Three perspectives.* New York, NY: Oxford University Press.

Mintzberg, H. (1979). *The structuring of organizations.* Englewood Cliffs, NJ: Prentice-Hall.

Mintzberg, H. (1983). *Power in and around organizations.* Englewood Cliffs, NJ: Prentice-Hall.

Pfeffer, J., & Salancik, G. R. (1978). *The external control of organizations: A resource dependence perspective.* New York: Harper & Row.

Schein, E. H. (2010). *Organizational culture and leadership* (4th ed.). San Francisco, CA: Jossey-Bass.

Shapiro, J. P., & Stefkovich, J. A. (2011). *Ethical leadership and decision making in education: Applying theoretical perspectives to complex dilemmas.* New York: Routledge.

Simpson, J., & Speake, J. (Eds.). (2008). *The Oxford dictionary of Proverbs* (5th ed.). Oxford: Oxford University Press.

Starratt, R. J. (2012). *Cultivating an ethical school.* New York: Routledge.

Stefkovich, J. A. (2006). *Best interests of the student: Applying ethical constructs to legal cases in education.* Mahwah, NJ: Lawrence Erlbaum Associates.

Woods, P. A. (2009). Nurturing democracy: Contribution of distributed leadership to a democratic organizational landscape. *Educational Management Administration & Leadership, 37*(4), 430–451.

Chapter 17

Mr. Murray vs. Merit Pay

Peter Brigg

Three weeks were left in the school year as the district administrators strolled into the administration building for their biweekly executive meetings. Stress levels were low with the state tests behind them. The pace was relaxed, and so was the attire for the principals in the district. Suits were replaced with golf shirts and khakis during the month of June. James Murray, principal of Lincoln Elementary, was looking forward to some summer downtime after his third year as a principal. He had yet another successful year, and was starting to emerge as a leader in the district.

The end-of-year executive meeting was always a reflective meeting based on the strengths and needs of the district. This year was no different. Dr. Hill, the superintendent of Barden School District (BSD), moved the meeting along quickly, providing data analysis of the district's test scores. He noted the students' adequate proficiency levels; however, test scores indicated that students were not meeting anticipated growth measures based on tests from the previous year. Dr. Hill continued, and began to reference incentivizing teachers. Murray knew exactly where he was taking the discussion, but he was shocked that Dr. Hill would implement a pay-for-performance system. To Murray, it was inconceivable that merit pay would be a driving force for the faculty in BSD. Hill started to describe a plan designed to provide merit pay to teachers based on student performance on the Pennsylvania state assessment. The rough outline described would provide teachers with the possibility to receive bonuses based on the percentages of students who achieved anticipated growth measures. Everyone in the district knew Murray to be ambitious. He came to BSD because he knew he could make a difference. His vision and work ethic paralleled the values of the district . . . until now.

Dr. Hill finished describing the incentive plan, and the room grew silent. Murray could not just sit there. He spoke up. He prefaced his comments by stating that he had nothing but respect for the superintendent, the board, and the decision-making process. He spoke from the heart, stating that he believed that it was his responsibility to give a voice to those who do not have one—his students. Murray spoke with passion, showing true advocacy for his students. Murray's words were well-articulated, despite the fact that this was the first time he had heard any notion of a pay-for-performance plan. The room of educators and central office personnel listened attentively. He concluded by stating that he would respect any decision that was made moving forward, but he needed to voice his opinion. Murray did not have time to truly analyze and weigh the outcomes. He felt a sense of urgency to speak his mind in front of his colleagues and superiors.

Silence ensued for approximately 30 seconds. Dr. Hill cleared his throat and said the following:

> James, that was well-stated; however, this is not up for debate. The board wants a merit pay system in place. There are more details to work out, and you are welcome to be part of the project development committee moving forward, but there will be a merit pay plan in place next year.

James saw this as a challenge and an opportunity. He agreed to be part of the committee, and he began doing his homework on the topic.

Murray spent many weekend hours gathering information regarding merit pay and the corresponding data, and sharing it with the committee. Murray remained objective in his discussions with the committee. He explained the advantages of merit pay programs, such as potentially recruiting and retaining more of the nation's intellectual minds; conversely, he explained the disadvantages, such as tension in the school environment and less collaboration. Murray provided the committee with research and findings on motivation and incentivized plans. Murray did not fear a collapse of BSD as an organization if such a system was implemented; however, BSD would not be a better organization for having implemented a merit pay system. While work is often synonymous with undesired and unengaging labor, Murray proved that having a passion for work is stimulating. As he developed an expertise on merit pay, the committee members became inspired and did the same.

Murray's passion, as well as his ability to remain humble and display humility, helped elevate his status as the leader of the committee. He did not pretend to have all of the answers. He sought out answers from mentors, friends, and those with more experience who were able to provide much-needed perspectives and value for a topic of which he had limited experience. Murray viewed this dilemma as an opportunity to learn and grow, while he also tried to keep the district on a path that remained in line with the current vision. His approach was admirable.

In Murray's eyes, incentivizing teachers through merit pay to raise standardized test scores was devaluing the efforts of his teachers and degrading the educational value established in the district. He knew he had to show the same kind of effort that he demands of his teachers and students. He spent a great deal of time gathering information about the topic and the district. He learned more about the board members and their ideals. He learned more about where and how the idea of merit pay developed among the board members. He learned more about the topic, including how other districts have fared when they implemented similar tactics. He looked at historical and longitudinal data on the district to determine if there had been previously attempted external reward systems, and the results of such systems.

At times, Murray presented information to the committee in ways that made it seem as though he was embracing merit pay; however, this approach was tactical. Murray made claims that it was possible to make performance pay work, but simply providing bonus monies would not suffice. In order for performance incentives to be effective, they must be based on student performance. Ensuring student success was the goal. Increasing student achievement must be the basis for all fundamental decision-making. There must be rewards or consequences embedded within the construct of the incentive plan. He assisted the committee members in understanding the complexity and challenges that come with implementing such a system. It would be easy and futile to state that incentivized teachers will work harder and produce better results. It was much more complicated than that. Murray explained that effort leads to performance, and when performance is measured, there will be a correlation to effort. Extrinsic motivators, such as merit pay, only last temporarily. Spiraling wages or bonuses can be motivating factors, but it will only motivate teachers to seek the next wages. In order for monetary incentive plans to be motivating, they would need to be constantly enhanced. Murray suggested that the district find another way to celebrate results.

Rumors of the potential plan made its way to the teachers in the district, and concerns of divisiveness and ethics arose among them. Tension among staff, and between staff and administrators, was imminent based on the reactions to the rumors. Murray spent a great deal of time listening throughout the process. He listened to the teachers and listened to the board. He listened when the committee was asked to develop, refine, and propose a merit pay system tied to student performance. He asked administrators their beliefs. He contacted districts that successfully implemented merit pay as well as districts that implemented and later removed incentive-pay plans. He asked community members. He discussed bonus systems within the corporate world, and again, he listened. He established a comfort level that allowed others to have a comfort level to speak openly and honestly. Teachers, administrators, and community members all appreciated his attentiveness and open-mindedness during their discussions. Murray gathered information in a way that was broad and thorough, and as a result, he found that he was sharpening his sword and improving his rhetoric.

A few weeks later, Murray requested time to meet with Dr. Hill and the rest of the school board members to present his findings. Murray knew that his position on merit pay would lead to tension; however, he was not naive to the fact that speaking out against the superintendent and school board directors would cause the tension to be placed directly on him. But he preferred the tension be between the board and himself rather than among the staff in his building.

Murray expected questions as he presented his findings. He expected difficult conversations. He did not expect the onslaught of challenging, condemning comments and attacks that took place; however, his passion did not allow the comments to deter him from his goal. His new-found vast wealth of knowledge on the topic projected him to a level of expertise that provided him with a comfort level not even Murray knew he had. Murray spoke passionately and impressively. He referenced data, research, and psychological implications. Murray had become an expert on incentive pay through his work as a member of the committee. It was clear he was the most knowledgeable on the topic, so his opinion had the most weight. The most evident and advantageous trait that he presented was his level of expertise. He was too well-versed on the topic for anyone to suggest that he was incorrect with his data or information.

Murray concluded his presentation by explaining that student achievement could only be reached if teachers believed in the shared vision set forth by the district. All stakeholders must believe in the same vision—a vision was the driving force, not bonus monies. The vision and intrinsic motivation would lead teachers to work toward increasing student achievement, not monetary rewards. Merit pay would not make teachers effective. Merit pay did not fit the vision of BSD. Merit pay was not indicative of the foundation on which BSD was built.

Murray's confidence did not waver throughout his presentation. He was diagnostic, analytical, and sensible. The board members challenged him, and he had a rebuttal. They asked questions, and he had answers. He was humble, but confident. Murray did not expect to convince each member of the board to dismiss the idea of incentive pay, and he certainly did not convince all of them; however, he was able to create a doubt in enough board members to convince them to at least put the plan on hold. All along, Murray kept the children at the heart of his decision-making process. He maintained his focus through every challenge presented to him, showing resiliency and grit through it all. He was fighting an uphill battle from the beginning.

Murray's approach demonstrated what democratic ethical leadership is: Ethics resides not in black or white judgment, but in a gray area. This gray area is the dilemma, a choice. There was no textbook that Murray could have read that would provide an answer about how to handle a situation such as this. Nothing was prescribed to Murray; however, he knew how to handle this situation because he knew and had already determined what was in the best interest of children long before he became a principal. The prescription for any dilemma is to do what is best for kids and stand up for what one believes in. Success in any leadership position is measured not by avoiding conflict, but by progressing in the face of challenges.

Murray managed the tension through empathy and respect. He had a clear direction, yet remained open-minded throughout the research he completed. As a leader, Murray recognized that he needed to be patient and appear objective under pressure in order to see this opportunity clearly, and to act on it virtuously. Murray remained mindful of the needs and desires of all stakeholders. He did not make ultimatums or act swiftly without having enough background knowledge to make a decision. He acted patiently and empathically throughout the process. Murray worked through the lens of a school leader—one that kept students at the heart of the decision-making process.

Questions to Discuss:

1. Who is the exemplar in this case? Describe.
2. What kind of leadership style did this exemplar exhibit?
3. Was there a critical incident in this story? If so, please discuss.
4. How did the exemplar deal with turbulence? Explain.
5. Which ethics did the exemplar turn to? Were these ethics appropriate and helpful to the decision-making process?

PART V

CAREER AS A CALLING

New DEEL Vision for Educational Leaders	Behavior of Conventional School Leaders
5. Sees one's career as a calling and has a well-developed sense of mission toward democratic social improvement that cuts across political, national, class, gender, racial, ethnic, and religious boundaries.	Sees one's career in terms of specific job titles with an aim to move to ever greater positions of perceived power within the current system's structure.

Reading the fifth New DEEL vision statement for educational leaders may raise an eyebrow or two. After all, the notion of following a calling might seem very old fashioned given our current emphasis on personal career advancement. But it is exactly this extreme form of career centeredness that causes us to promote a different value in the form of a calling. We believe that following one's calling is a rich, lifelong alternative that is potentially liberating for each of us. Yet, how one goes about finding and following a calling raises serious questions that merit some examination.

Self-knowledge is a quality of individuals who have found their calling. Just the word *calling* evokes images of listening and reflection, patience and earnestness. Ironically, though it is a path starting with the self, it is the opposite of self-absorption, since the intention is to serve and thereby connect to others. Those who follow a calling have imagined a world that is a complex tapestry of which they are an interwoven thread, connected in some way to all of the other strands. It is this awareness that makes the crumbling of old barriers between people not merely logical, but almost obvious. How can we be woven into the same tapestry and not be of a piece? Being of a piece means our concern for self cannot be alienated from our concern for all. If this is so, how can we not see our calling as a mission rooted in democratic social improvement for everyone, if these are aspirations we have for ourselves?

Therefore, making a commitment to something larger than self seems a logical outgrowth of self-knowledge. Horace Mann, who more than any other individual established the public education system in the U.S., is an exemplar of this pattern. As Cremin observed:

> Mann's school was to be common, not in the traditional European sense of a school for the common people, but in a new sense of a school common to all people. It was to be available and equal to all, part of the birthright of every American child. It was to be for rich and poor alike, not only free but the equivalent in quality of any comparable private institution. In it would mix the children of all creeds, classes, and backgrounds, the warm association of childhood kindling a spirit of mutual amity and respect which the strains and cleavages of adult life could never destroy. In social harmony, then, Mann found the primary goal of the school.
>
> (Cremin, 1979, p. 8)

Ella Flagg Young presents another example. She is remembered for becoming Superintendent of Chicago's schools in the early 20th century, thereby being the first woman to lead a major city school system in the U.S. But even a cursory review of her life's work shows that it was the cause of expanding an effective and caring educational system that held the center ground: "Just 17 years old when she began as a primary teacher in a ghetto school in Chicago, for the next half century, Young devoted her life to improving the quality of education for students and teachers" (Webb & McCarthy, 1998, p. 223).

Probing oneself deeply and connecting one's calling to the welfare of others is the start of a lifelong journey. There are constant trials, so understanding the power of the long game is essential. Because those following a calling are in the process of becoming, they accept the fact that they will never arrive at a destination. Looking at their lives carefully, they will see evidence that their progress is never linear and is often marked by setbacks. Contemporary calls for grit and resilience reflect the same need for perseverance (Duckworth, Peterson, Matthews, & Kelly, 2007). Perhaps the life of Malala Yousafzai is our best current example of these qualities in action in her struggle for women's right to an education.

Aung San Suu Kyi is a clear case in point. Although internationally renowned and the winner of numerous honors, including the Nobel Peace Prize, she experienced harsh challenges, including 15 years of house arrest. Due to her confinement, she could not be with her husband in England while he was dying. None of these challenges dissuaded her from her goal of democracy in Burma:

> But the Burmese have never had the luxury of despair: After all, it was their country, their future, their destiny, and however slim the hope of change, it was all they had to cling to. Suu, with her calm resolve, was the embodiment of that slim, stubborn hope. Steadfastness: That was the example Suu set for her fellow citizens. And now, almost miraculously, it is beginning to receive its reward.
>
> (Popham, 2012, p. 400)

Yet the aim of Aung San Suu Kyi's mission seems as universal as it is focused on her homeland. We can see the same pattern in the life of Nelson Mandela, who suffered greatly in prison for many years before leading South Africa out of apartheid and into democracy.

Although less well known, Kyrgyzstan's Kurmanjan Datka also belongs to this group. Kurmanjan rose from obscurity into national leadership in the mid-19th century, a time of Russian annexation and domination. Finding a path between capitulation on the one hand and suicidal rebellion on the other, she guided her people through turbulence and multiple challenges to their survival. Like Suu, she paid a heavy personal price for leadership—having lost children in the struggle, and even having to witness the execution of her favorite son while preventing a doomed rescue attempt.

But knowing that a calling sets a person on a long-term mission is not the same as settling for undying, quiet waiting for a better time to simply appear. In a recently discovered speech given in April 1965 at UCLA, Martin Luther King Jr. warned that merely waiting for times to change would not solve anything, because those opposing change also used that time to resist. For King, playing the long game did not mean resigning to endless, neutral waiting in numbed passivity, just as peaceful nonviolence itself was not passive. It meant using time to work, struggle, and realize the goals of that mission, piece by piece, throughout one's life, and to pass that calling on to a following generation. The inspiring rhetoric of King's speech was matched with a specific request for volunteers from his audience to join in efforts to help African Americans in the South to register to vote.

A calling often takes the form of voyages beyond home to meet new people, challenging old assumptions through dialogue and thereby preventing one's mission from ossifying.

Russell Conwell, founder and first president of Temple University, kept that university afloat for many years by crisscrossing the nation to deliver his famous Acres of Diamonds lecture. The funds Conwell raised in over 5,000 iterations of this address were vital to Temple's early survival. But the community he created throughout the U.S. was equally critical. Whether

near to Philadelphia or across the continent, Conwell always made a point
to connect with local people and learn from them:

> I visit a town or city, and try to arrive there early enough to see the postmas-
> ter, the barber, the keeper of the hotel, the principal of the schools, and the
> ministers of some of the churches, and then go into some of the factories and
> stores, and talk with the people and get into sympathy with the local condi-
> tions of that town or city.
>
> (Conwell, 1915, p. 2)

The message of Acres of Diamonds is that we can all take better advantage of our own situation, wherever that is, to improve life for ourselves and
our communities. By his willingness to venture out and connect to such
diverse groups of people, Conwell expanded his own perspective and kept
his vision fresh.

There is a wizened optimism found in those following a calling, even if
their goals seem beyond reach to others. As Archibald MacLeish said of the
poet Carl Sandberg, "those who are credulous about the destiny of man,
who believe more than they can prove of the future of the human race, will
make that future, shape that destiny" (MacLeish, 1969, p. xxii).

This calling, in its largest sense, transcends one's own career; and it is
not limited to one's personal aspirations, but crosses the boundaries of self,
place, and even time. In contrast to a personal careerist climb, community
is a necessity, not a distraction. Others are not competitors for coveted roles
in a pyramid scheme of competitive advancement but essential partners
in building a future worthy of ourselves and our heirs. In this way, those
following a calling avoid heroic leadership in favor of humility and quiet
power.

As inspiring as these women and men are, following a calling that connects one to the wider world in pursuit of democracy and social justice is
not the sole province of the famous. It is a choice available to anyone who
wishes to be so oriented. It is a gift to be shared. Some may say that we are
asking too much of educators. In an era of intense accountability and its
subsequent burdens, we are asking that educators do all of that work *and*
fathom their characters to such depths that they transform what was a job
into a calling connected to a lifelong mission. We take the view that seeking
a calling is empowering, inspiring, and transforming. The chapters in Part
V further amplify that assertion.

Anthony Normore and Jeffrey Brooks write about Viktor Frankl, who
was not a traditional educator. However, through his book *Man's Search for
Meaning* (Frankl, 2006), he displayed a resilience and desire for personal
freedom that should serve as an inspiration to us all. Despite being a prisoner at Auschwitz, Frankl kept his ability to respond to horrid situations

in such a way that he maintained his self-respect and inner freedom, and he was not crushed by the Nazis. He held on to his love of democracy and was able to transcend political, national, ethnic, and religious boundaries. Frankl was an exemplar who exhibited the moral courage to combat staggering injustices. Normore and Brooks believe that Viktor Frankl is someone whom contemporary educators should try to emulate.

Marla Susman Israel, in the following chapter, writes about an extremely effective superintendent: Dr. Jane Brenner, who was faced with changing demographics in her school district. When Brenner first took over the district, her students spoke 30 different languages. Ten years later, they spoke 60 different languages. While Dr. Brenner provided faculty development in English language learner (ELL) and special education, what was needed was something more. She saw the connection between parental education and that of her students; and through perseverance, she persuaded important constituencies and stakeholders to understand the need for an ELL Parent Center. Here was a leader who was able to transcend boundaries, particularly of social class, race, ethnicity, and religion, to educate diverse students and their families.

Christopher Branson, Michele Morrison, and Rachael McNae write of an urban school principal, Cliff, who works in New Zealand. Cliff was committed to social equity, financial equity, and cultural equity. One of his accomplishments was to create a more equitable basketball event, keeping the needs of his lower-income students in mind. He also developed professional justice by providing equal benefits and equal accountability to elementary and secondary teachers. Cliff was a leader who expected and accepted criticism, but he also had enough confidence to believe he was on the right path to achieving social and professional justice for his students and teachers.

Roger Barascout, in the final chapter in Part V, focuses on Kevin Jennings, a bullied boy growing up in poverty. Despite his challenging upbringing, Kevin as an adult worked to change the climate for LGBT young people. Against all odds and with help from his mother, Kevin was able to graduate from Harvard. He went on to form the Gay, Lesbian & Straight Education Network (GLSEN) and eventually became an advisor to U.S. presidents, providing them with ways to make schools safe places for diverse students. His work crossed boundaries of human differences, and his passion for developing safe schools never ceased.

REFERENCES

Conwell, R. H. (1915). *Acres of diamonds.* New York: Harper Brothers.
Cremin, L. A. (1979). *The republic and the school: Horace Mann on the education of free men.* New York: Teachers College Press.

Duckworth, A.L., Peterson, C., Matthews, M.D., & Kelly, D.R. (2007). Grit: Perseverance and passion for long-term goals. *Journal of Personality and Social Psychology, 92*(6), 1087–1101.

Frankl, V.E. (2006). *Man's search for meaning.* Boston, MA: Beacon Press.

MacLeish, A. (1969). *Introduction to* The Complete Poems of Carl Sandburg. New York: Harcourt Brace Jovanovich.

Popham, P. (2012). *The lady and the peacock: The life of Aung San Suu Kyi.* New York: The Experiment.

Webb, L. D., & McCarthy, M. M. (1998). Ella Flagg Young: Pioneer of democratic school administration. *Educational Administration Quarterly, 34*(2), 223–242.

Chapter 18

The Moral Courage of Viktor E. Frankl

An Exemplary Leader

Anthony H. Normore and Jeffrey S. Brooks

Critical incidents define each of our lives, and when leaders make ethical decisions, they affect the lives of those around them (Brooks & Normore, 2005). When we were asked to contribute a chapter to this book, we reflected on the many critical incidents we have experienced, studied, and read about, and considered the impact that leaders had on our behavior and thinking. Our charge was then to consider which, of all the possible leaders, has had the most profound impact on our personal and professional lives—who did we consider the most influential, and why?

We thought about numerous influential teachers, administrators, students, scholars, humanitarians, novelists, ethicists, political figures, cultural figures, and other people who fit the bill—those who have been role models in our own lives. Some are famous, and some are not. The one commonality is that they each had a profound effect on who we are as human beings, as educators, as educational leaders, and as citizens and public servants who have a responsibility to the world (Paul-Dosher & Normore, 2008; Starratt, 2004). Further, each has a moral commitment to high-quality learning in one form or other—a commitment based on three essential virtues: proactive responsibility; personal and professional authenticity; and an affirming, critical, and enabling presence to the workers and the work involved in teaching and learning (see Starratt, 2004). Included in the litany of highly influential people who have helped shape our lives—whether through literature, prose, narratives, crusades, or humanitarian efforts—include, but by no means are limited to the following: Wangari Maathai, Aristotle, Charles Dickens, Voltaire, Atticus Finch, Mother Teresa, Harriet Tubman, Dr. Martin Luther King, Florence Nightingale, José Rizal, Nelson Mandela, Philippe Pinel, the Dalai Lama, Mohandas Gandhi, John Howard,

Edna Gladney, Fannie Lou Hamer, Siddhartha Gautama, and many more. Although we can unequivocally state without question the positive impact of these people who have helped shape us, we decided we would dedicate this chapter to Viktor E. Frankl.

WHY VIKTOR E. FRANKL?

Both of us were moved to personal and professional change after reading Frankl's 2006 book, *Man's Search for Meaning*, in which he documents his experiences as an Auschwitz concentration camp inmate during World War II. He explains the sources of strength that allowed him to survive Nazi extermination policies and concentration camps. His account is less about his work and what he suffered and lost, and more about the source of his strength and will to survive. For us, one of his most enduring insights is when he discusses freedom in relation to locus of control: "Forces beyond our control can take away everything you possess except one thing, your freedom to choose how you will respond to the situation" (Frankl, 2006, p. x). As educators, we sometimes find ourselves faced with unreasonable polices and public perceptions that affect how well we teach, the content we deliver, the learning of those we teach, the level of respect for the profession, or the emotional destruction of people who live on society's margins. We face complex, sometimes ambiguous challenges. As a result, we sometimes feel our circumstances are insurmountable, that we are defeated, or that we have run out of choices. Frankl would have argued that "we are never left with nothing as long as we retain the freedom to choose how we will respond" (Frankl, 2006, p. xi).

We do not pretend to compare our work to the experiences of Frankl. However, we do believe the foundation of our work resonates with Frankl's mission and purpose in writing *Man's Search for Meaning*—the human side, the compassionate side, the resilient side, and the purpose-driven aspects of leadership and learning (Brooks & Normore, 2005). Frankl was guided by moral courage and an inner sense of responsibility for social development. Like Frankl, we see our careers as a calling—one where we believe we have worked hard to develop a sense of moral courage, responsibility, a mission toward democratic social improvement, and a vision that transcends political, national, class, gender, racial, ethnic, and religious boundaries.

MORAL COURAGE: "DOING THE RIGHT THING"

Scholars have long argued about the definition of "courage" through their works (e.g., Aristotle, 1962; Block & Drucker, 1992; Coles, 2000; Miller, 2000; Putman, 1997). According to Miller (2005, p. 1), "courage is something we all admire." Miller further asserts that when asked to describe courage, most people think about an individual running into a burning building, or maybe a fictional hero saving the day . . . but when asked to go deeper, to really define courage, the only response that comes to mind is "I know it when I see it" (Miller, 2005, p. 2). We use the word "courage" to honor the firefighters, rescue workers, and police officers who ran into the twin towers on 9/11. We also use the word "courage" to honor the individuals who blow the whistle on corporate corruption. As emphasized by Miller, the two cases are very different: "In the first case the individual's very life was in jeopardy by the physical actions being performed; in the second case the individuals risked their jobs by telling the truth" (Miller, 2005, p. 3). The point is that heroes come from all walks of life, and they put themselves at direct and indirect risk in order to help others.

It is natural to have doubts throughout our lifetime. Our fears are real. Our aspirations and achievements are real, too. We are sometimes uncertain about our abilities to make decisions in the face of dilemmas (Shapiro & Gross, 2013; Shapiro & Stefkovich, 2011). When we do, we sometimes turn to Frankl's experiences and reflect about his uncanny ability to make calm and magnanimous decisions in the face of danger and uncertainty—to have moral courage to take a stand against injustice when he had everything to lose. We might learn a great deal from his psychotherapeutic method, which involved identifying a purpose in life to feel positively about, and then immersively imagining that outcome. According to Frankl, "the way a prisoner imagined the future affected his longevity" (Frankl, 2006, pp. 57–58).

Frankl persevered in order to effect serious change. He dealt with arduous and torturous situations in a search for meaning and purpose while clinging to hope, democracy, and morality based on his own sense of courage and principles. Frankl concluded that the meaning of life is found in every moment of living; life never ceases to have meaning, even in suffering and death. He further concludes that:

> A prisoner's psychological reactions are not solely the result of the conditions of his life, but also from the freedom of choice he always has even in severe suffering. The inner hold a prisoner has on his spiritual self relies on having a hope in the future, and that once a prisoner loses that hope, he is doomed.
>
> (Frankl, 2006, p. 112)

FINAL REFLECTIONS

Among the lessons we have learned from Viktor Frankl are the following: What is really needed is a fundamental change in our attitude toward life.

First, we need to reflect deeply on our beliefs and character in order to learn more about the outer world. Second, we must ultimately realize that *it does not really matter what we expect from life, but rather what our ethical nature demands of us in a given situation*. Third, reflection must come first, but then learning, research, and action must follow—put differently (paraphrasing Gurdijieff), to know better is not sufficient to do better. As Frankl urges:

> Our question must consist, not in talk and meditation, but in right action and in right conduct. Life ultimately means taking the responsibility to find the right answer to its problems and to fulfill the tasks which it constantly sets for each individual.
>
> (Frankl, 2004, p. 77)

As professors, we take great pride in our work and reflect constantly on our responsibility to act with moral courage in school and university. Though we struggle from time to time, we realize we are fortunate to have happiness, contentment, and freedom in our personal and professional lives. We are motivated by the moral courage of those like Viktor E. Frankl, whose attitude, perseverance, discipline, and fight for "what is right and just" inspire us to appreciate our freedom and to fight for those whose freedom is denied or imperiled. We do not pretend to have the moral courage or strength of character of Frankl, but like him—inspired by him—our meaning in life is to help others find freedom.

Questions to Discuss:

1. As the authors of this chapter question: Why Victor Frankl? Why choose him as an exemplar for educational leaders? Discuss.
2. What was the critical incident or critical incidences that Frankl faced?
3. What was the turbulence level in this situation? Provide some details.
4. What kinds of ethical beliefs did Frankl hold? And how did he maintain those ethics in incredibly trying times?
5. How does Frankl's writings relate to the democratic social improvement of our current society, taking into account all kinds of diversity?

REFERENCES

Aristotle (1962). *Nicomachean Ethics* (M. Ostwald, Trans.). Indianapolis, IN: Bobbs-Merrill.

Block, G., & Drucker, M. (1992). *Rescuers: Portraits of moral courage in the Holocaust.* New York: TV Books.

Brooks, J.S., & Normore, A.H. (2005). An Aristotelian framework for the development of ethical leadership. *University Council for Educational Administration (UCEA), Journal of Values and Ethics in Educational Administration, 3*(2), 1–8.

Coles, R. (2000). *Lives of moral leadership.* New York: Random House.

Frankl, V.E. (2004). *On therapy of mental disorders: An introduction to logotherapy and existential analysis* (J.M. DuBois, Trans.). London: Brunner-Routledge.

Frankl, V.E. (2006). *Man's search for meaning.* Boston, MA: Beacon Press.

Miller, R. (2005). *Moral courage: Definition and development.* Arlington, VA: Ethics Resource Center.

Miller, W.I. (2000). *The mystery of courage.* Cambridge, MA: Harvard University Press.

Paul-Doscher, S., & Normore, A.H. (2008). The moral agency of the educational leader in times of national crisis and conflict. *Journal of School Leadership, 18*(1), 8–42.

Putman, D. (1997). Psychological courage. *Philosophy, Psychiatry & Psychology, 4*(1), 1.

Shapiro, J.P., & Gross, S. (2013). *Ethical educational leadership in turbulent times: (Re) solving moral dilemmas.* New York: Routledge/Taylor & Francis.

Shapiro, J.P., & Stefkovich, J. (2011). *Ethical leadership and decision making in education: Applying theoretical perspectives to complex dilemmas* (3rd ed.). New York: Routledge/Taylor & Francis.

Starratt, R. (2004). *Ethical leadership.* San Francisco, CA: Jossey-Bass.

Chapter 19

A Question of Resources

How Should Public Education Funds Be Spent?

Marla Susman Israel

INTRODUCTION

This chapter tells the story of Superintendent Jane Brenner, who displays a "well-developed sense of mission toward democratic social improvement that cuts across political, national, class, gender, racial, ethnic, and religious boundaries" (Gross, 2012). This exemplar is not the traditional "hero," but rather is a consummate educational professional who has done the ethically challenging work that is asked of educational leadership on a daily basis.

THE SUPERINTENDENT AND CASE DISTRICT

Dr. Jane Brenner began her career as an educator teaching math and science at a residential treatment facility for behaviorally disturbed girls who were wards of the state. Jane taught at this center for 18 months until it closed due to lack of funding. Jane earned a master's degree focusing on special education. She then taught middle school students in special education for five years. In 1986, she became a middle school assistant principal and subsequently ascended to the principal role (1990–1999), and she earned her doctorate in 1995. In 1999, she became an elementary principal in a northern suburb outside a large Midwestern city. She quickly ascended to the assistant superintendent position from 2002–2004; and then in 2004, she was named the superintendent, where she remained until 2014.

Dr. Brenner's K–8 school district was comprised of 1,750 students in three elementary schools and one middle school. The district had approximately

300 faculty members, of which 150 were certified and 150 were classified. This school district, which had always considered itself diverse, experienced dramatic demographic shifts in population.

In 2004, 30 languages were represented in the district. Next to English, Korean and Russian were spoken most often. Many of these families were primarily well-educated professionals. Approximately 10% of the district's population was considered low income as determined by the free and reduced lunch program.

By 2014, the district had over 60 languages, with the largest growing population from Mexico, followed by Asian immigrants from Pakistan and parts of India. The Black population appeared to have stabilized around 11%. The Asian population in its entirety was 36%, and the Caucasian native-born population was around 33%. Most striking, however, was the low-income demographic that had climbed to 56%. The district now had a minority-majority (56% whose first language was not English) and an English as a Second Language (ESL) department that served more students than the entire district's special education department.

Unlike other school districts that had floundered under similar demographic shifts (Knierim, 2013), during 2004–2014 this district was able to remain financially solid, and it had students performing well on standardized measures. It also became a leader in providing equity and access to students and their families, regardless of language or income level (Scheidenhelm & Milligan, 2010). Rather than luck, resolute leadership played an important role.

THE CRITICAL INCIDENT AND INITIATIVE

Dr. Jane Brenner was well acquainted with the shifting demographics of her school district. She was aware of the challenges that neighboring school districts within the township were facing. With the increasing diversity of student language groups and the increasing poverty levels of these families, she knew that maintaining the status quo would not be successful.

Understanding the changing needs of her students, Dr. Brenner began a complex set of instructional initiatives during the years of 2004–2008, such as full-day kindergarten, an aggressive program of professional development for teachers, and a revision of the curriculum, to ensure that all students had equity and access to the core curriculum. This type of instructional leadership is what is consistent with attributes of successful superintendents (Waters & Marzano, 2006; Young & Mawhinney, 2012).

However, Dr. Brenner felt she had to do more than just lead within her own district's schools. She perceived that there was "turbulence" within her own district and throughout the township that needed to be addressed (Shapiro & Gross, 2013). In particular, Brenner felt compelled to create a new approach to increasing parent engagement, district- and township-wide, with purposeful planning (Collins, 2005; Fullan, 2010). Therefore, the township's new collaborative initiative was focused on engaging parents of the English language learner (ELL) students. In her words, "many of whom were ELL adults who did not have a voice in their children's education and did not know how to engage with the American public school system" (J. Brenner, personal communication, December 20, 2012). Drawing on research that parent involvement is one of the greatest predictors of student achievement across all demographic sub-groups and socio-economic sub-groups (Ingram, Wolfe & Liberman, 2007; Smit & Driessen, 2007; Vera & Israel et. al., 2012), Jane Brenner was determined to create a township ELL Parent Center, funded by public schools funds.

Brenner first began the process leading to an ELL Parent Center through a series of focus groups comprised of a wide variety of stakeholders, including community organizers, librarians, municipal officers, school board members, ELL teachers, administrators and concerned parents. Over a series of months, these focus groups met to tease out the concept of an ELL Parent Center funded by public school monies heretofore earmarked for direct services to children. A funding formula was devised pro-rating each district's share by the size of the district participating. These monies would pay for the rent of the space located in Dr. Brenner's district office. A subgroup of township superintendents framed out a proposal and presented it to their respective boards in 2008 with the mission of "Helping Parents Help Their Children" (ELL Parent Center, 2008). Upon initial board approval, federal and state grant proposals were written and secured, providing resources to pay for an ELL Center Coordinator and to create a fund balance that could generate interest and allow for the Center to grow and be sustainable. By 2009, seven out of nine school districts within the township had signed the inter-governmental agreement to make the ELL Center a reality.

After the first two years of operation, a local university conducted an evaluation of the ELL Center and wrote a comprehensive report detailing the accomplishments of the Center and future steps for improvement. Another evaluation by the same university was written two years later. By January 2012, all nine districts had signed the inter-governmental agreement for the ELL Parent Center, ensuring that all parents within the township (PK–12) who had children attending any of the nine township school districts could avail themselves of parent education services. To date, these services include but are not limited to: English classes enabling parents to engage with American public schools (Parents as Educational Partners), citizenship classes, know your community classes sponsored by the village bus system (taking families to the library or police stations), resume writing, birth-through-three healthy learning classes, interpreter training classes, networking groups for Latino families, support groups for immigrant mothers and their adolescent daughters, and professional development and leadership development (where parents receive a small stipend) so that these parents can become real partners in the schools and serve as liaisons throughout the community as new families move in.

As Dr. Brenner states:

> The ethical piece behind all of this and the challenge was in convincing our communities, and some needed more convincing than others, that local tax dollars are well spent directed toward parent programming with a direct link to the public schools. We did this (I led the charge on this) because we believed we had a professional responsibility to respond to the needs of our community.
>
> (J. Brenner, personal communication, December 20, 2013)

WHAT IS LEFT UNSAID BUT MUST BE UNCOVERED

While this vignette may give the illusion of a linear and smooth journey, it was one filled with "moderate to severe turbulence" (Shapiro & Gross, 2013, p. 16). Brenner had to invest her own time and her own resources to make the ELL Center a reality, as she was the face of the initiative and the writer of the grants (Kouzes & Posner, 2012; Watkins, 2003). She had to lead difficult conversations throughout the township during a period of great economic unrest and within an anti-immigrant environment (Spielman, 2013). It is important to note that two of the aforementioned ELL Center program offerings focus on earning one's citizenship and resume writing—two topics that can prove to be most contentious when the established white majority is out of work (Apple, 2010).

Additionally, Dr. Brenner was open to critique, allowing herself to be vulnerable by hosting two external evaluations during the Center's growth process (Starratt, 2012). This meant that while Brenner was building a coalition to get all nine districts within the township involved and to maintain current support within her own district, she encouraged dissenting voices to help build a program and did not let those voices deter from the work. Brenner brought diverse constituencies together around a common vision.

Brenner had to convince these constituents that while a causal link has yet to be found between educating the parents of ELL students and an improvement in student outcomes, the expenditure of public money was still the right thing to do. Brenner's actions were driven by moral courage and vision. She confronted the possibilities of criticism and loss of her job with the "understanding of the meaning of the values in which she fought for and the importance of ethics both in human life and in the life of organizations and communities" (Gini & Green, 2013, p. 55). Jane Brenner demonstrated that living her values was possible without compromising either her ethics or career. She retired on a high note, cherished by the township, her school district, and her community. This exemplar is best concluded with Dr. Brenner's own words:

> It's the role of the superintendent, the leader, to mirror back to the board what the needs of the district are and make recommendations based on these core set of values. It's the job of the leader to articulate those values back out to the school district, because if decisions in the school district are made grounded in those values then decisions will be consistent and have a foundation. And whether or not a board retains that leader is neither here nor there. I've been fortunate, but I don't think I've ever wavered from this set of core values about why I'm doing the work I'm doing.
>
> (J. Brenner, personal communication, December 20, 2013)

Questions to Discuss:

1. Would you consider Superintendent Jane Brenner to be an exemplar? Why or why not?
2. What was the critical incident or critical incidences that made Dr. Brenner move towards changes in her district?
3. What kinds of changes did Dr. Brenner believe were necessary for this district in order to create democratic social improvement?
4. Was turbulence involved in this case? If so, what kind of turbulence? And how did Dr. Brenner increase or decrease it?
5. What kinds of ethics did Dr. Brenner hold? Illustrate how she made decisions using the ethics of justice, care, critique, or profession.

REFERENCES

Apple, L. (2010). Anti-illegal immigration group endorses local candidates. *Chicago Reader*. Retrieved March 1, 2014, from http://www.chicagoreader.com/Bleader/archives/2010/08/26

Collins, J. (2005). *Good to great and the social sectors: A monograph to accompany "Good to Great."* New York: Harper Collins.

ELL Parent Center. (2008). Mission statement. Retrieved March 23, 2014, from http://www.ellparentcenter.org/#!

Fullan, M. (2010). *All systems go: The change imperative for whole system reform.* Thousand Oaks, CA: Corwin Press.

Gini, A., & Green, R. M. (2013). *10 virtues of outstanding leaders: Leadership & character.* Malden, MA: Wiley-Blackwell.

Gross, S. (2012). A new DEEL for our future. *New DEEL.* Retrieved March 22, 2014, from https://sites.temple.edu/newdeel

Ingram, M., Wolfe, R. B., & Lieberman, J. M. (2007). The role of parents in high-achieving schools serving low-income, at risk populations. *Education and Urban Society, 39,* 479–497.

Knierim, A. (2013, June). How much money does Illinois have? We don't know. *Huffington Post.* Retrieved March 23, 2014, from https://www.huffingtonpost.com/anthony-knierim

Kouzes, J., & Posner, B. (2012). *The leadership challenge.* (5th ed.). San Francisco, CA: Jossey-Bass.

Scheidenhelm, C., & Milligan, S. (2010). *ELL Center External Reviewer's Report.* Evanston, IL: Office of Learning Technologies and Assessment.

Shapiro, J., & Gross, S. (2013). *Ethical educational leadership in turbulent times: (Re) solving moral dilemmas* (2nd ed.). New York: Routledge.

Smit, F., & Driessen, G. (2007). Parents and schools as partners in a multicultural, multi-religious society. *Journal of Empirical Theology, 20,* 1–20.

Spielman, F. (2013). Chicago's finances among the worst after 2008 recession: Study. *Chicago Sun-Times.* Retrieved March 1, 2014, from http://www.suntimes.com/23606034-761

Starratt, R. J. (2012). *Cultivating an ethical school.* New York: Routledge.

Vera, E., Israel, M. S., Knight, L., & Goldberger, N. (2012). Exploring school involvement in parents of English language learners. *School Community Journal, 22*(2), 183–202.

Waters, J. T., & Marzano, R. J. (2006). *School district leadership that works: The effect of superintendent leadership on student achievement.* Denver, CO: Mid-continent Research for Education and Learning.

Watkins, M. (2003). *The first 90 days: Critical success strategies for new leaders at all levels.* Boston, MA: Harvard Business School Press.

Young, M. D., & Mawhinney, H. (Eds.). (2012). *The research base supporting the ELCC standards: Grounding leadership preparation & educational leadership constituent council standards.* Washington, DC: Council of Chief State of School Officers.

Chapter 20

In Search of Seamless Education

Christopher M. Branson, Michele Morrison, and Rachel McNae

Cliff has been a school principal in New Zealand for some 27 years. His first three principal appointments were to rural primary (elementary) schools. This positive experience of leading primary schools led him to successfully apply for the position of principal at a rural Area (K to 13) School, because he was attracted by its claim to provide a seamless educational culture. Currently, Cliff is the principal of a large urban co-educational secondary (years 9 to 13) state-funded school, which caters to 12-to-18-year-old students. Although each of these appointments was contextually unique, two key features—social and professional justice—have consistently influenced Cliff's educational leadership practice.

A commitment to social justice became an essential ingredient in Cliff's professional practice, right from his early years as a principal. More specifically, in Cliff's own words, "it's really about equity—social equity, financial equity, cultural equity." Just prior to his first principal appointment, he had become so appalled by the diverse and oppressive inequities within the South African social and political apartheid system that he became passionately committed to explicitly opposing issues of perceived social injustice in his own country of New Zealand. Thus, Cliff became an avid public protestor and demonstrator against an international rugby tour by a South African team to New Zealand, despite being a devout rugby fan. This seamless alignment of attitude and action in Cliff's character was further strengthened during the 1980s by his explicit stance, along with many others, against the perceived inequities inherent in the then New Zealand government's proposed educational reforms outlined in its "Tomorrow Schools" (Ministry of Education, 1989) report. Arguably, the successful outcomes achieved in both of these difficult and complex situations fortified Cliff's conviction that not only can social injustices be overcome through strategic and determined action, but also that there is great personal meaning and satisfaction to be gained by doing so. For Cliff, "there's nothing more rewarding than making a difference and that's not about manipulating the environment but creating [more equitable] conditions." A truly meaningful commitment to redressing social injustice is about making real, rather than superficial, changes that remove inequities in the lives of those who are often powerless to do this on their own accord.

A prime example of this conviction was reflected not only in Cliff's choice of schools to lead, but also in his action against a regional basketball association. Cliff consistently chose to apply for principal positions in low-decile schools. In New Zealand, as introduced by the national government in 1995, each school is assigned a "decile" rating. A decile is an averaged measure of each school community's socio-economic deprivation, calculated on the basis of an accumulated evaluation across this community of household income, parental occupation and educational qualifications, household crowding, and income support. Decile 1 schools have the highest percentage of students living in socio-economic deprivation, as defined by this accumulated evaluation, while decile 10 schools have the lowest percentage. His current school is classified as a decile 4 school. For Cliff, such schools provide the opportunity to make a real difference—"it's not about lowering the standard, it's about finding different ways to get to the standard." Without help, often students in low-decile schools are not able to find these different ways to learn and achieve, and so they remain locked in underachievement and thus, ultimately, underemployment and poverty.

One of the ways in which Cliff's current school community raises the aspirations and achievement of its students is through engagement in formal community sporting competitions—in particular, basketball. As Chapman and West-Burnham stridently argue:

> If equality and well-being are not central to practice, they will be seen as the marginal rather than a fundamental part of the learning process. This fragmentation of physical, social growth and intellectual development can only weaken connections and impoverish the learning experience.
>
> (Chapman and West-Burnham, 2010, p. 20)

For Cliff, the opportunity for the students to be involved in a challenging but enjoyable basketball competition provided them with a key source of self-confidence and self-esteem not regularly experienced in their academic endeavours. However, the annual competition fees collected by the regional Association to organize the interschool basketball competition were becoming exorbitant—yet the actual quality of the competition was diminishing. Most of these fees were being used to support the Association's elite regional team's financial demands, and little of it was being used to support and encourage the interschool competition. Rather than just accepting this situation, Cliff took affirmative practical action. Initially, he sought a better deal for the schools from the Association, but to no avail. Hence, Cliff took it upon himself to contact other school principals and basketball coaches in order to organize an "independent" interschool basketball competition, which not only required far less financial outlay from each competing school, but also enabled all of the money to be directed towards supporting and advancing this particular competition. Despite the Association labeling this as an "unsanctioned event", the competition prospered, and Cliff's response to the Association's threats was that its competition "was not fair, so what do you do, you do something about it. So you're either part of the problem or part of the solution. There's no part in between." As McNae (2014) states, "coming to understand social justice leadership as a way of being, a practice that embodies the personal and seeks to disrupt the political, is not easy work" (p. 108). Cliff illustrated significant commitment to being part of the solution and addressing this through his deliberate and planned actions.

In Cliff's mind, positive relationships are at the heart of creating a socially just community. Positive relationships create "transparency—people know what your expectations are and they know what outcome is possible." It is only through the establishment of positive relationships that you can authentically know what is in the best interests of another person and to know what is suitable help for this person. Chapman and West-Burnham (2010) describe this perspective as "social pedagogy", as it is said to "reconcile and integrate the academic with the cultural, the intellectual with emotional, and personal with the social" (p. 152). But herein lies the challenge for any school trying to build and maintain a culture formed upon positive relationships. "The quality of relationships—that whole issue of putting it right and if you stuff up a relationship it's not good enough; it's not good enough to be a bully, and that comes from [the teachers] as well, and the kids know that there's some accountability for the teachers." Often in low-decile schools, it is the teachers who have the most to learn about how to relate positively and transparently with the students (Bishop & Glynn, 1999; Bishop, Ladwig, & Berryman, 2013). Just as Cliff's school introduced restorative practices as an alternative to punitive consequences for unacceptable student behavior, it also applied restorative practices to teachers who thoughtlessly deal with students. "Nothing destroys relationship more quickly than inconsistent or inequitable accountabilities." Moreover, in Cliff's opinion, it is not uncommon for teachers to demand more from their students in this regard than they do of themselves, and this is not acceptable. However, he continues to see the school as a place of opportunity for all students at his school. Cliff's intentions are similar to the guiding words of bell hooks:

> The classroom, with all its limitations, remains a location of possibility. In that field of possibility we have the opportunity to labor for freedom, to demand of our comrades, and ourselves an openness of mind and heart that allows us to face reality.
>
> (hooks, 1994, p. 207)

The second of Cliff's two key features of his educational leadership practice is that of professional justice. Here, professional justice encompasses a commitment to equitable professional expectations of each and every teacher in the school. In alignment with the view proposed by Dantley and Tillman (2006), as a leader for social justice, Cliff felt compelled to interrogate and rectify policies and practices that shaped his schools towards perpetuating professional inequalities and marginalization. Initially, this feature was formed during Cliff's first principalship appointment to a two-teacher (teaching principal plus one other teacher), low-decile school. In such a context, "there's no excuses—if the kids didn't achieve, it was our fault." It soon became obvious that the only way for the students in this school to achieve was for both Cliff and the other teacher to work together to learn from each other, to improve each other, and to become the best teacher that each could be. A key action of this socially just educational leader was the ability to reflect upon the needs of the community and the direction the school must take to ensure appropriate provision for all (Furman, 2012).

However, this outcome became a more universal feature of Cliff's leadership practice during his time as the principal of the Area School. The school's claim of providing a seamless educational environment seemed to be unfounded, particularly "because there's two collective agreements in New Zealand, one primary and one secondary, . . . all the secondary teachers got [workload and resourcing] rewards yet two thirds of the kids were in the primary area and these teachers got an eighth of the reward units and so performance was an issue." Under Cliff's leadership, it was expected that each and every teacher would have the same professional accountabilities along with the same professional benefits, regardless of their level or area of teaching. From a practical perspective, this meant that because "primary teachers got no release and secondary teachers got a lot, I made the secondary teachers do the primary school release, so they got a good perception about facilitating high quality learning."

This commitment to professional justice continues to be a distinguishing feature at Cliff's current school. It begins with cooperative learning for teachers, both within and across curriculum areas, whereby each teacher is first challenged to explore the theory and practice of a particular pedagogical perspective in a generic sense; but then the teacher is expected to discuss his or her resultant new professional learning with the teacher's respective subject area colleagues. Moreover, key expert teachers from within the school largely lead this form of professional learning. But next comes, from Cliff's perspective, the critically important phase of professional accountability. As he explains:

> Essentially the indicator of poor performance is often poor planning and therefore each teacher has to produce evidence of interaction with a cohort of kids, so you just can't give me a unit plan and a weekly plan—you've got to give me some evidence to indicate how you will teach effectively . . . So the whole idea is to provide a tangible way for the teacher to identify the precursors to good classroom interaction. Then the curriculum leader can have a really constructive conversation with the teacher about their teaching and the students' learning. Following this, the curriculum leader meets with the Deputy Principal and me to discuss these conversations. I then meet with each teacher to discuss his or her teaching and ongoing professional development.

But there is a formidable side to the establishment of professional justice based upon rigorous and consistent accountability. Not every teacher will willingly and readily attend to, or meet, the required expectations. Thus, if these are to be consistently realised, the principal needs to be committed and resilient enough to follow through with all necessary steps to, firstly, support the teacher, but ultimately, to cease the teacher's employment if necessary. Cliff has had to take this later course of action on seven occasions, with one case taking some five years to be processed through the various legal systems, "but it was really about demanding performance outcomes."

Being passionate and committed towards what matters in a school is rarely easy, but it is rewarding. For Cliff, resilience, optimism, and enjoyment comes from "being confident in what I am doing while, at the same time, knowing that I can't be friends with my staff. Having other professional goals keeps me occupied and confident and those sorts of things." Moreover, confidence is enhanced though following previously established and clearly articulated processes:

> Often people don't follow processes because it's a difficult decision, but that's exactly why they have processes, to help you with difficult decisions. When you don't follow processes things often become unresolved over a period of time and they fester.

As a result of his relentless commitment to social and professional justice, Cliff "loves coming to work. I enjoy it. I mean, it's about helping people grow, and I think I make a positive difference."

Questions to Discuss:

1. Would you consider Cliff to be an exemplar? If so, why? If not, why not?
2. What leadership beliefs did Cliff hold? Did he lead using those beliefs? Discuss.
3. Were there any critical incidences in this case? If so, explain.
4. What kinds of turbulence occurred in this case? Did Cliff manage to decrease or increase the turbulence?
5. What did Cliff mean by social justice and professional justice? What kinds of ethics was he describing?

REFERENCES

Bishop, R., & Glynn, T. (1999). *Culture counts: Changing power relations in education.* Palmerston North, NZ: Dunmore Press.
Bishop, R., Ladwig, J., & Berryman, M. (2013). The centrality of relationships for pedagogy: The Whanaungatanga thesis. *American Educational Research Journal, 20*(10), 1–31. doi:10.3102/0002831213510019
Chapman, L., & West-Burnham, J. (2010). *Education for social justice: Achieving wellbeing for all.* London: Continuum International.
Dantley, M. E., & Tillman, L. C. (2006). Social justice and moral transformative leadership. In C. Marshall & M. Oliva (Eds.), *Leadership for social justice: Making revolutions in education* (pp. 16–30). Boston: Pearson Education.
Furman, G. (2012). Social justice leadership as praxis: Developing capacities through preparation programs. *Education Administration Quarterly, 48*(2), 191–229. doi:10.1177/0013161X11427394
hooks, b. (1994). *Teaching to transgress: Education as the practice of freedom.* New York: Routledge.
McNae, R. (2014). Seeking social justice. In C. Branson & S. Gross (Eds.), *Handbook of ethical educational leadership* (pp. 358–369). New York: Routledge.
Ministry of Education. (1989). *Tomorrow's schools: The reform of education administration in New Zealand.* Wellington, NZ: Author.

Chapter 21

A Bullied Boy Who Grew Up to Change School Climate

Roger Barascout

> *Do not accept something that is wrong. Stand up, push for change, and don't quit until you get it!*
>
> —Kevin Jennings, Farewell Address, GLSEN Respect Awards 2008[1]

As a young boy, Kevin Jennings discovered that going shopping for a new trailer with his mom was one of the great thrills of his childhood. Walking around the trailer park to choose a new home was, to Jennings, what going to a toy store would be for any other eight-year-old boy, except he got to live in his new "toy." Jennings' experience growing up in poverty as an itinerant preacher's son and being forced to endure school bullying made his passion for social justice and equality become his mission in life—a mission that has changed the school climate for LGBT (Lesbian, Gay, Bisexual, and Transgender) youth in the United States.

Kevin Brett Jennings was born on May 8, 1963, in Fort Lauderdale, Florida, to Chester and Alice Jennings. He was the youngest of five children—his siblings included one girl and three boys—and seven years younger than his nearest sibling. Jennings was an avid learner, while his brothers excelled at sports; and between his brothers' and his dad's example, they set the standard for masculinity he had to fit. This defined masculinity would become a constant inner battle for Jennings into his adult life, as well as the fundamentalist values his family held regarding righteous living as the sole path to salvation. This religious philosophy was shared by Jennings' extended family, some of whom were also members of the Ku Klux Klan. Jennings' father refused an invitation to join the Klan, and soon after moved the family to a trailer park in Weldon and later in Lewisville, both in North Carolina, the latter where Jennings spent most of his childhood.

The day Jennings turned eight, his dad passed away. At the funeral, Jennings' mom fainted, and the terrorized young boy began to cry. It was at this moment that one of his brothers taught him a life lesson that would leave a mark on him for many years: "Don't cry. Be a man. Don't be a faggot." Being a "real man" meant never showing emotions or weakness, even if you were eight and at your dad's funeral. And any male who deviated from those standards had a name. That name was *faggot*.

If that was the first time Jennings was called a faggot, it was certainly not the last time. Jennings started to be bullied in first grade, when he was called "queer" for the first time. It was the beginning of years of being increasingly bullied on a daily basis. It led him to hate recess, as he would choose books over football, and hence be called sissy or queer; and to avoid unstructured settings like the lunchroom. He was the target of the sissy and faggot taunts in fifth grade during the hour-long bus rides to and from school. By sixth grade, he was also bullied by boys in the trailer park, where he was then living with his mom. Since his cousins and brothers didn't live in the trailer park, he didn't have close friends to play with, and the only solution to deal with the constant harassment was to avoid going outside. The unconscious consequence was a weight-gaining sedentary life in which Jennings fell into the vicious cycle of feeling unhappy—and the unhappier he was, the more he used food as a coping mechanism. So he was called faggot at school and "Baloney Boy" by his brothers.

But Jennings' experience with bullying reached new heights when, during his last years in junior high, he felt there was nowhere to turn. Some of his teachers joined the harassment or simply stood by and let it happen. Jennings decided that reporting it to the school guidance counselor would alleviate his problems. When Jennings detailed and listed names of the bullies, the counselor simply responded, "I find it hard to believe this stuff happens and teachers do nothing about it," and, "I know those kids. They are good kids. I don't believe they'd do something like this."

Jennings refused to go back to school on his first day of tenth grade unless he'd be transferred to another school. Amazingly, his mom did the impossible and enrolled him at a school for gifted students. At the new school, Jennings "started to remember his name was 'Kevin' and not 'faggot.'" He was finally celebrated for his academic accomplishments. In his senior year of high school, his teachers encouraged him to apply to the most prestigious Ivy League colleges in the nation. He was in disbelief when the acceptance letter came from Harvard. He was going to be the first one in his entire family to go to college, and he would do so at one of the most prestigious schools in the world.

After Jennings graduated *magna cum laude* with a bachelor's in history, he took a job as a history teacher at a school in Rhode Island, and soon after, at a boarding and day school in Massachusetts. It was in the latter where he disclosed his sexuality to the school community. As a result, Jennings mentored the first straight-gay alliance in the United States, in 1988, at the request of a straight female student.

"I figured out how to be a teacher by thinking back to the worst teachers I had in school," Jennings has said. His forced definition of masculinity and insensitive school personnel were the main motivators to fight for inclusion, diversity, and educational innovation, and to become a champion for anti-bullying. Jennings was not going to "stand by while ignorance and bigotry toward gay people ran rampant in the school." So he decided teachers needed to know how to address these issues. With two other colleagues, he founded what years later became GLSEN (the Gay, Lesbian & Straight Education Network), the first nonprofit of its kind, that "strives to assure that each member of every school community is valued and respected regardless of sexual orientation or gender identity/expression."[2] It provided support to teachers—and eventually to students, school administrators, and parents—with information, nonacademic activities, and even suggestions for curricula, so that teachers and students would be better prepared to create a safe school climate of equality and respect that was conducive to learning and personal growth.

In 1999, GLSEN conducted the first "National School Climate Survey to examine school-specific experiences of LGBT-identified youth nationally."[3] One year later, the same survey revealed similar results as the study from two years prior. A major finding was that for many of the nation's LGBT youth, school was an unsafe and even dangerous place. It also showed that the majority of the youth reported being verbally harassed or experienced incidents of physical harassment, physical assault, and sexual harassment. And more surprisingly, it revealed that the homophobic remarks were frequently heard from faculty and staff. By 2011, the same study showed a decline in anti-LGBT language and a significant decrease in victimization based on sexual orientation.[4] GLSEN has continued to expand nationally, with activities and programs such as the National Day of Silence, and No-Name Calling Week. In 2008, ten years after the creation of the first straight-gay alliance, there were over 4,200 straight-gay alliances in the United States; and that year, 7,700 high schools participated in the National Day of Silence, a 50% increase from the year before.[5]

But Jennings' advocacy for the safety of schools went even further. In 1992, he was invited to chair the Massachusetts governor's newly created Commission on Gay and Lesbian Youth. After many hearings and much research, the Commission made five recommendations to the governor, who endorsed four of them: policies protecting gay and lesbian students from harassment; training for school personnel; school-based clubs support groups; and school-based counseling for family members of gay and lesbian students. In 1993, the state board of education voted unanimously to make the four recommendations the official policy of the state of Massachusetts, and a line item was put in the education budget to create a program to implement the new policy. By 2008, when Jennings stepped down as Executive Director of GLSEN, there were 11 states that protected students from bullying and harassment based on sexual orientation, and six more had been added by 2013. What Jennings had always envisioned had become a reality.

Jennings' tireless work and commitment to improving school safety brought him an invitation to the White House in the early 1990s, to be one of 12 community leaders to discuss with President Clinton the issues faced by the LGBT community. The scared eight-year-old boy called "faggot" on a daily basis was sitting next to the President of the United States, and advising him on matters that affected the nation.

President Clinton was not the only president who called Jennings. From 2009 to 2011, Jennings was appointed Assistant Deputy Secretary and Director of the Department of Education's Office of Safe and Drug-Free Schools (OSDFS) by President Barrack Obama. Both the President and Jennings were criticized by conservatives for the appointment of an openly homosexual activist. But despite all the public attacks against Jennings, he was able to create an unprecedented level of attention and energy to fighting bullying in a way never before done in the United States.[6] "If a school isn't a safe place for all students, and some are harassed and bullied for being different, academic achievement suffers tremendously,"[7] Jennings has said. That has been the motto behind his work: promoting not just respect and equality, but also safe learning environments for all students.

The boy who used to be excited about choosing a new trailer home grew up to sit next to and give advice to presidents, and to transform the laws and policies that affect the education system of the United States. Kevin Jennings' mission has crossed political, national, class, gender, racial, ethnic, and religious boundaries. Jennings and his husband Jeff continue working to bring about a world where anyone can grow to who they are and share in "liberty and justice for all."

Question to Discuss:

1. Do you think of Kevin Jennings as an exemplar? If so, why? It not, why not?
2. What was the leadership style Jennings used? Was it appropriate for him? Discuss.

3. What was the critical incident in this story? What happened to get Jennings through this incident?

4. What kind of ethics did Jennings display? Did he turn to the ethic of justice, critique, care, and/or the profession? Why did he choose this or these ethics?

5. What was the turbulence level for Jennings as he began 10th grade? Who brought the turbulence level down for him? How was this accomplished? What did Jennings do as an adult to bring down the turbulence level for others?

NOTES

1   Unless otherwise specified, all quotes are from K. Jennings (2006), *Mama's boy, preacher's son*, Boston, MA: Beacon Press.

2   GLSEN mission retrieved from the GLSEN website (2014), http://glsen.org/learn/about-glsen

3   GLSEN (2001). The 2001 National School Climate Survey. Retrieved from http://glsen.org/sites/default/files/2001%20National%20School%20Climate%20Survey%20Full%20Report.pdf

4   GLSEN (2011). The 2011 National School Climate Survey Executive Summary. Retrieved from http://glsen.org/sites/default/files/2011%20National%20School%20Climate%20Survey%20Executive%20Summary.pdf

5   Jennings, K. (2008). GLSEN Respect Awards Farewell Speech. Retrieved from http://www.youtube.com/watch?v=OSkve3CJctk

6   Schulman, J. (2011, June 17). Kevin Jennings to critics: "You completely failed." *Media Matters for America*. Retrieved from http://mediamatters.org/blog/2011/06/17/kevin-jennings-to-critics-you-completely-failed/180656

7   Long, C. (2006). An Interview With Kevin Jennings, Founder of GLSEN. *National Education Association (NEA)*. Retrieved from http://www.nea.org/tools/30428.htm

Conclusion: Sharing Values, Theories, Praxis, Curriculum, and Pedagogy

INTRODUCTION[1]

The New DEEL was developed to move away from the current reform approaches for public school improvement, which are based primarily on test results and accountability, and instead turn to a values approach that emphasizes social justice and social responsibility. The New DEEL reclaims school reform by advocating for democratic ethical leadership in education. Despite the current inequality of wealth and opportunity in American society, New DEEL members believe that all of our public schools, from pre-K through secondary education, need to inspire truly democratic, ethical, participatory cultures and values that will ultimately produce outstanding citizens.

One way to inculcate the values of social justice and social responsibility is through the creation of new courses for educational leaders that merge theories with praxis. In this way, cohorts of school leaders will be prepared to resolve the challenging and complex educational issues of this era. They will be able to face paradoxical situations and make difficult and wise, ethical, and democratic decisions.

Another approach we believe is essential is to focus on experiential learning. Through autobiography, personal and professional codes, debates, and other important individual and shared activities, students will begin to understand their own values and those of others. Additionally, students, who are expected to develop their own reflective and analytical ethical dilemmas can better understand their own behavior and how they have approached problems in the past. Through self-analysis of their own actions, they can determine what they value and improve their problem-solving abilities. These activities can help to prepare them to become more rational as well as compassionate human beings. It can also lead to the development of transformative leadership capabilities rather than maintain transactional ones.

This final section of the book will focus on values, theories, praxis, curriculum, and pedagogy. It is meant to provide help, especially for instructors using this book in their classes. Further guidance is provided by googling: New DEEL. There the reader will find a website designed with two sections that might be especially useful. One section is under the heading Curriculum, and the other section is under Scholarship. These categories will provide models for those faculty members who wish to utilize New DEEL courses and writings.

THE CURRICULUM: MERGING THEORIES WITH PRAXIS

In the preparation of New DEEL transformative school administrators, it is important that courses are developed that take into account ethics and democracy. One such course, *Ethical Educational Leadership*, was designed by Shapiro, originally in the early 1990s. (See the New DEEL website for a recent course syllabus.) She created this course at Temple University for aspiring and current educational leaders to focus on more than the ethics of justice and care. These two ethics had been emphasized in the writings of Strike, Haller, and Soltis (1988) during this period. Originally, she utilized fictional ethical dilemmas that could be found in the books of the era. Over time, however, she and her colleague, Jacqueline Stefkovich (formerly at Temple and now at The Pennsylvania State University), encouraged their graduate students, who were also practitioners, to develop their own ethical dilemmas that were authentic, coming from their classrooms and their institutions.

Shapiro and Stefkovich (2011) eventually developed theory and combined it with authentic dilemmas from the field. In their book entitled *Ethical Leadership and Decision Making in Education: Applying Theoretical Perspectives to Complex Dilemmas*, now going into its 4th edition, they presented the Multiple Ethical Paradigms (MEP) of justice, critique, care, and the profession. (See the Introduction to Part IV for an in-depth description of MEP.) However, it should be noted that MEP is only one model for the preparation of ethical leaders (e.g., Begley and Johansson, 2003; Branson, 2014; Gross, 2014; Shapiro and Gross, 2013; Starratt, 1994, 2004; Stefkovich, 2014; Tuana, 2014).

While Shapiro and Stefkovich were developing the MEP model, Steve Gross was working on his own theory. In his books *Staying Centered: Curriculum Leadership in a Turbulent Era* and *Promises Kept: Sustaining School and*

District Leadership in Turbulent Times (1998, 2004), Gross found that sites that had developed curriculum, instructional, and assessment innovations for several years had all experienced some degree of turbulence or volatile conditions. Further, he discovered that the degree of turbulence at the ten schools and districts he had studied could be divided into four levels: light, moderate, severe, and extreme. He created these levels using the pilot's metaphor for turbulence. In later writings (Gross, 2014; Shapiro and Gross, 2013), Gross deepened his Turbulence Theory by adding the concepts of positionality (where one sits in relation to a given turbulent event), cascading (the impact of surrounding turbulent events on any new shock), and stability (the extent to which a person or organization can or cannot rely on previous performance or reputation during a turbulent event). See the Introduction to Part II for a more detailed description of his theory.

Turbulence Theory, therefore, gives educational leaders an enhanced ability to calibrate the severity of the issue at hand. It further aids them in attempting to contextualize a given problem as they construct strategies to move to less troubled waters.

THE MERGING OF TWO THEORIES WITH PRAXIS

While much of Gross' early work on Turbulence Theory was used to help explain the behavior of school leaders facing organizational challenges, he realized after speaking with Shapiro that there was an application of his work in the realm of ethical decision-making. Those facing ethical dilemmas in the midst of busy organizational lives need to respond in a deeply reflective, systematic fashion as well as take into account the emotional context of the decision making. For these purposes, Gross and Shapiro connected the MEP model, consisting of the ethics of justice, critique, care, and the profession, with Turbulence Theory in their scholarship, when working with field practitioners, and when advising university and state officials. In this context, the four levels of turbulence—light, moderate, severe, and extreme—are used early in the process to help illuminate the degree of disruption represented by the dilemma.

Positionality of individuals and cascading events enter into the reflections as well in an effort to stabilize certain situations. Thereafter, an analysis of the problem through the perspective of the combined ethical lenses takes place, followed by a course of action. At the conclusion of this process, a second estimate of turbulence is conducted, given that course of action. It can be asked, 'If I take this course of action, where might turbulence be as a result, and for whom?'

Combining two theories, the MEP with Turbulence Theory, has proven to be very helpful to aspiring and current educational leaders. They now have the ability to gauge a situation, deal with it from an emotional perspective utilizing Turbulence Theory, and then use the MEP to assist them in making an ethical decision. This combination of theories with praxis and emotions with reason has enabled aspiring educational leaders to practice, in the safety of the classroom, how to deal with the challenges they face in their schools and higher education institutions. This focus on the preparation of ethical leaders is a strong aspect of the New DEEL reform movement.

To provide some deep understanding of the attributes and behaviors of a New DEEL leader, Gross designed an innovative course for educational leaders. He entitled it *Profiles in Democratic Ethical Leadership*. (See the syllabus on the New DEEL website under Courses.) He wanted this course to illustrate properties of the New DEEL movement, focusing on democracy as well as ethics. This course functions as a research project in spirit and function. Specifically, the class seeks to answer this question: What are the underlying qualities that make an individual a democratic, ethical leader? Rather than employing a didactic and deductive process of imposing a definition upon students, his approach follows an inductive process patterned after Bruner's (1974) concept attainment model. Using a wide cross-section of women and men from the U.S. and around the world, both in our own time and from time past, the class considers the common qualities these leaders demonstrate as they faced their greatest personal and professional challenge. Some of these leaders come directly from the field of education, such as John Dewey and Ella Flagg Young. Others were identified from different professions, such as Desmond Tutu and Aung San Suu Kyi. Individuals such as these have had a major impact on society and have, therefore, shaped education. The class considers this inductive study of leaders and constructs a vibrant and organic definition of democratic ethical leadership that will inform their practice.

Yet another New DEEL course has been very recently designed by Gross. It is entitled *Educational Reform*. Although the title is familiar, the approach is far different from the traditional reform course. Gross' approach consists of three integrated activities: debate, lecture/discussion, and engagement. In this innovative course, Gross asks students to think of themselves as joining an educational reform task force. He expects them to answer the following questions as the course moves along:

- What are the structural natures of reform in American educational history? Are we speaking about one reform movement or about various political/philosophic movements that use the word "reform" for their own ends?
- How have the educational reform movements evolved over the past twenty years?

- What role have special interests such as business and universities played in educational reform?
- Where does educational reform seem headed in the near term and long-range future? What might be our choices? How might this play out at the building level?

Students are asked to formulate an individual development plan for themselves. Each student will need to:

- Describe the New DEEL Vision for Educational Leadership that currently matters most to him or her.
- Make an estimate of where the student is regarding his or her leadership using the New DEEL Vision (far along, in between, or early days?).
- Write a plan for the student's own development as an education leader, including:
  1. Readings
  2. Professional Development and experiences the student would like
  3. Support the student will need (examples: mentoring, joining organizations)
  4. Create a budget and a time line for this process

As a culminating activity, student teams take one of the New DEEL Vision statements for Educational Leaders and connect it to the larger context of education reform. The goal is to help refine the model by illustrating how it works in actual practice. Students present their work at the New DEEL conference, thereby sharing their growing expertise with the community of scholars and practitioners in attendance.

PEDAGOGY

To make this book meaningful as well as student- and instructor-friendly, you have no doubt noted that questions were provided at the end of each chapter. These questions will hopefully enable you to delve into the strengths and weaknesses of the exemplars. The questions focused on: an explanation of why this individual was an exemplar; a description of what leadership style the exemplar displayed; a discussion of the critical incident/s that the exemplar faced; a description of what kind of ethic/s the exemplar utilized; and an explanation of the kind of turbulence that was displayed and how the exemplar dealt with it.

The hope is that these questions will be discussed, along with others emerging from the students and from you, the instructor, and might form the basis of group activities. One way to do this is by breaking the class down into small groups. Each group of students could be asked to choose a facilitator to watch the clock and keep the discussion moving, and a recorder to be ready to synthesize the answers to the questions at the end of each chapter for the group. The recorder should not only focus on the majority decisions of the group, but should also comment on those who have stated a minority opinion. In this way, most of the voices of the group will be heard. In addition, it is important that facilitators and recorders change so that all students have a chance to be discussion leaders and scribes.

While you are reading this book, we suggest that the instructors in your institution provide other related learning experiences for their students. One approach that we recommend is asking students to write about their own lives, indicating times when they displayed some aspect of transformative leadership or wished they had done so. They could also highlight critical incidences in their stories when they acted in ways they believed were admirable despite high levels of turbulence, or discuss what they could have done in their own challenging circumstances after reading the lives of these exemplars.

Beside autobiography, we think it is important for students to write about an exemplar they admire. These exemplars could be famous individuals, but they could also be relatives, friends, teachers, and religious leaders from their local communities. They would then be expected to write an essay about why and in what ways these individuals inspired them. If there were critical incidences that these exemplars faced, they should be included. Students could also make presentations, enabling the class to turn to a more constructivist approach. Through these presentations, the students could determine the direction that the class would take, since the selected exemplars will vary from semester to semester.

After the students discussed the values that their exemplars exhibited, another activity could be for the students to write their own personal and professional ethical codes. They could then discuss their own beliefs in light of one or more of the exemplars in this book. In particular, it might be helpful to highlight the different kinds of ethics that the exemplars used compared to their own codes to determine if the ethics of justice, critique, care, and the profession were part of their value system—or if only one or two ethics were turned to by the exemplars and by the students in the class. In this way, the MEP could be discussed.

It is hoped that when the students' exemplars and their critical incidences are discussed, the turbulence level will be indicated. It is important for the students to determine if the exemplar heightened or lowered the turbulence level when faced with challenges, and to explain why he or she did so. It is also worthwhile to discuss the concepts of positionality, cascading, and stability.

IN CONCLUSION

We hope that you have found this book to be useful in the development of transformative educational leaders. We believe that the New DEEL Vision of Educational Leadership can provide some guidance into the kind of educational administrator needed in the current era. Hopefully, it will provide some legitimacy for those of you who wish to reclaim reform. This can be done through the analysis of the lives of exemplars in different times and under diverse circumstances who have been influential in modifying education in their own societies and eras. It can also be done by self-reflection of your own decisions and behaviors. It is hard to take stands that go against the tide, and most of these exemplars have been challenged and have struggled. Despite the odds, they have managed to make major achievements. We hope they will inspire students to move towards transformational leadership.

Given the pressures of today's policy environment, educational administrators may believe they are trapped in the position of conventional or transactional leadership. Our hope is that the cases in this text combined with the questions posed for each of them, as well as the possibility of new curriculum and pedagogy, will help all of us find intermediate steps leading to a more positive professional life. We also hope that those of you who begin to take steps towards the New DEEL Vision of Educational Leadership will sense the difference in your institutions as faculty begin to feel more appreciated, and as students see themselves as individuals and not as numbers on standardized tests.

Rather than being subdued by the current educational reform agenda, we hope that the exemplars in this book will provide the pioneering spirit needed for all of us to move forward towards the new vision of educational leadership. It is hard to challenge the status quo, but one step at a time can make the difference and can help to create a better world—a world of social justice and social responsibility.

NOTE

1 Some of this chapter comes, in part, from J. P. Shapiro and S. J. Gross (2013), Part I, Chapter 1.

REFERENCES

Begley, P. T., & Johansson, O. (Eds.). (2003). *The ethical dimensions of school leadership.* Boston, MA: Kluwer Academic.

Branson, C. M. (2014). The power of personal values. In C. M. Branson & S. J. Gross (Eds.), *Handbook of ethical educational leadership* (pp. 195–209). New York: Routledge.

Bruner, J. (1974). *Going beyond the information given.* New York: Norton.

Gross, S. J. (1998). *Staying centered: Curriculum leadership in a turbulent era.* Alexandria, VA: Association for Supervision and Curriculum Development.

Gross, S. J. (2004). *Promises kept: Sustaining innovative curriculum leadership.* Alexandria, VA: Association for Supervision and Curriculum Development.

Gross, S. J. (2014). Using turbulence theory to guide actions. In C. M. Branson & S. J. Gross (Eds.), *Handbook of ethical educational leadership* (pp. 246–262). New York: Routledge.

Shapiro, J. P., & Gross, S. J. (2013). *Ethical educational leadership in turbulent times: (Re) solving moral dilemmas* (2nd ed.). New York: Routledge.

Shapiro, J. P., & Stefkovich, J. A. (2011). *Ethical leadership and decision making in education: Applying theoretical perspectives to complex dilemmas* (3rd ed.). New York: Routledge.

Starratt, R. J. (1994). *Building an ethical school.* London: Falmer Press.

Starratt, R. J. (2004). *Ethical leadership.* San Francisco, CA: Jossey-Bass.

Stefkovich, J. A. (2014). *Applying ethical constructs to legal cases: The best interests of the student* (2nd ed.). New York: Routledge.

Strike, K. A., Haller, E. J., & Soltis, J. F. (1988). *The Ethics of School Administration.* New York: Teachers College Press.

Tuana, N. (2014). An ethical leadership development framework. In C. M. Branson & S. J. Gross (Eds.), *Handbook of ethical educational leadership* (pp. 151–175). New York: Routledge.

Author Biographies

Steven Jay Gross is Professor of Educational Leadership and Founding Director of the New DEEL Community Network at Temple University. Gross' teaching, books, articles, and research activities focus on initiating and sustaining democratic reform in schools and Turbulence Theory. His books include: *The Handbook on Ethical Educational Leadership* (2014, coedited with Christopher Branson), *Ethical Educational Leadership in Turbulent Times* (2013, coauthored with Joan P. Shapiro), *Leadership Mentoring* (2006), *Staying Centered: Curriculum Leadership in a Turbulent Era* (1998), and *Promises Kept: Sustaining School and District Leadership in a Turbulent Era* (2004).

Gross served as Editor of ASCD's *Curriculum Handbook* series and as a Senior Fellow at the Vermont Society for the Study of Education. Gross also served as Chief of Curriculum and Instruction for the State of Vermont, Associate Professor of Education at Trinity College of Vermont, and Curriculum and Staff Development Director for the Rutland Northeast Supervisory Union in Vermont.

Gross has been Distinguished Visiting Research Scholar (Australian Catholic University), Routledge's Author of the Month, and is on the roster of the Fulbright Specialist Program. Gross is the recipient of the Willower Award for Excellence and the University Council for Educational Administration's Master Professor Award.

Joan Poliner Shapiro is Professor of Higher Education and Co-director of the New DEEL Community Network at Temple University. Previously, she served as Associate Dean and Chair of Educational Leadership and

Policy Studies in Temple's College of Education and as President of Temple University's Faculty Senate. She also has been Co-director of the Women's Studies Program at the University of Pennsylvania, supervised intern teachers, and taught middle school and high school in the United States and United Kingdom.

In the area of scholarship, Shapiro has coauthored: *Reframing Diversity in Education* with Trevor E. Sewell and Joseph P. DuCette (Rowman & Littlefield, 2001); *Gender in Urban Education* with Alice E. Ginsberg and Shirley P. Brown (Heinemann, 2004); *Ethical Educational Leadership in Turbulent Times* (2nd ed.) with Steven Jay Gross (Routledge, 2013); and *Ethical Leadership and Decision Making in Education* (4th ed.) with Jacqueline A. Stefkovich (Routledge, forthcoming). She has also written more than sixty journal articles and book chapters.

Shapiro is the recipient of Temple University College of Education's Outstanding Teacher Award, the Willower Award of Excellence, the Lindback Foundation Distinguished Teaching Award, the University Council of Educational Administration's Master Professor Award, Routledge's Author of the Month, and Temple University's Great Teacher Award.

CONTRIBUTOR BIOGRAPHIES

Quisar Abdullah is an adjunct faculty member at Temple University, where he teaches undergraduate courses on Leadership and Communication, Research Methods, Conflict Resolution, and Organizational Communication. He also teaches a graduate course on Innovation, Technology and Teaching in Higher Education. Full-time, he serves as the Assistant Director and Quality Assurance Manager for Client Services at Temple University. He holds a B.A. in Political Science and Religion and an M.Ed. in Adult and Organizational Development, and he is currently pursuing a Ph.D. in Educational Psychology at Temple University. His chapter "Muslim Leader Formation and Education" was published in 2012 by SAGE in *Religious Leadership: A Reference Handbook*.

Judith Aiken is Associate Professor of Educational Leadership at the University of Vermont. Dr. Aiken directs the Doctoral Program in Educational Leadership and Policy Studies. Her writing interests center on the development of educational leaders with a focus on ethical, social justice practices. She teaches courses in leadership, curriculum, and supervision, and oversees the Administrative Licensure Internship Program for school principals. Her work has appeared in the *Journal of*

School Leadership, Planning and Changing: An Educational Leadership and Policy Journal, the *Journal of Leadership Studies,* and *Educational Leadership Review.* She has contributed numerous book chapters and coedited a book published by IAP titled *Social Justice Leadership for a Global World.*

Roger Barascout, after a brief but active career in opera, returned to higher education administration, working in student services, academics, and alumni affairs. His dissertation on donor giving behavior motivated him to assist nonprofit arts organizations with their development and donor relation strategies. In addition, Dr. Barascout currently works in Strategic Initiatives for the Fox School of Business at Temple University, and he maintains permanent lectureships at both the National Conservatory and the Escuela Superior de Música in Guatemala.

Lynne Blair earned her Bachelor of Arts in Mathematics from Bucknell University. After three years of teaching high school mathematics, Dr. Blair earned her master's degree in school counseling from the University of Pennsylvania. She was a high school guidance counselor for eight years before becoming an Assistant Principal and now Principal. She earned her Doctorate in Educational Leadership from Temple University. Her dissertation focused on a character education program that built resilience and a sense of community in a suburban high school.

Christopher M. Branson is the National Head of Education in the Faculty of Education and Arts at the Australian Catholic University and was the Executive Director of the University Council for Educational Administration (UCEA) Center for the Study of Leadership and Ethics from 2011 to 2014. His research interests include the nature and practice of leadership, ethical leadership, educational leadership, personal and organizational values, and organizational change. He is the sole author of two books, Leadership for an Age of Wisdom and Leading Educational Change Wisely, and a coeditor of the Handbook of Ethical Educational Leadership.

Marc Brasof is an Assistant Professor of Education at Arcadia University's School of Education. Dr. Brasof has received several awards, including the 2012 Pennsylvania Council for Social Studies Outstanding Program of Excellence Award; the 2011 Pennsylvania Council for Social Studies Outstanding Social Studies Project Award; the 2011 New Democratic Ethical Educational Leadership Award for Outstanding Contribution; and the 2009 Christian R. and Mary F. Lindback Award for Distinguished High School Educators. Dr. Brasof's research interests include student voice, distributed and democratic leadership, and organizational learning. In *Student Voice and School Governance: Distributing Leadership to Youth and Adults* (forthcoming), Dr. Brasof expands on work presented in this volume.

Peter Brigg is the Principal of Sabold Elementary in Springfield School District in Pennsylvania. He is an experienced educator who has held numerous positions at the elementary level. He became an administrator after seven years in the classroom. Mr. Brigg earned his undergraduate degree at Widener University and a master's degree in Educational Leadership from Villanova University. He is now pursuing a doctoral degree at Temple University. Mr. Brigg is an inspirational leader who is committed to excellence for his school and community.

Jeffrey S. Brooks is Professor of Educational Leadership and Chair of the Department of Leadership and Counseling at the University of Idaho. Dr. Brooks' research focuses broadly on educational leadership, and he examines the way leaders influence (and are influenced by) dynamics such as racism, globalization, social justice, and school reform.

Barbara S. Di Toro, a New DEEL member since 2008, is Associate Director of Temple University Music Preparatory (noncredit division of the Boyer College of Music and Dance), and an adjunct music faculty member at Arcadia University. Her classroom experiences include teaching music at the collegiate, elementary, and preschool levels. Barbara is the New DEEL Assistant Director for Website Development and serves on the boards of the Temple University Alumni Association, the Boyer College Alumni Association, and Children's Opera Box. Her degrees include an Ed.D. in Educational Administration, graduate and undergraduate degrees in music (Temple University), and a B.A. in elementary education (Holy Family University).

Patricia A. L. Ehrensal is an Assistant Professor of Educational Administration at the College of New Jersey. She received her Ed.D. in educational administration from Temple University. She has authored articles and book chapters examining ethics, law, the social construction of children, and the organizational arrangements of schools. She was the guest editor of a special edition of the *Journal of School Leadership* on law and ethics.

Fenwick W. English is the R. Wendell Eaves Senior Distinguished Professor of Educational Leadership in the School of Education at the University of North Carolina at Chapel Hill. He has written thirty-six books and numerous book chapters, and he has refereed many journal articles. In addition, he served as General Editor for the 2005 *SAGE Handbook of Educational Leadership;* the 2006 *SAGE Encyclopedia of Educational Leadership* *and Administration*; and the 2009 SAGE Major Works Series in *Educational Leadership and Administration*. His most recent text is *The Art of Educational Leadership* (2008) released by SAGE. He served as President of UCEA from 2006–07, and later President of the National Council for Professors of Educational Administration (NCPEA) from 2011–12. He received the NCPEA's Living Legend Award.

William C. Frick is an Associate Professor in the Department of Educational Leadership and Policy Studies, Jeannine Rainbolt College of Education, University of Oklahoma. He holds a Ph.D. in educational theory and policy from Pennsylvania State University. His prior work experience includes fourteen years in the public schools as a teacher, school counselor, principal, and director of curriculum and instruction. A recent publication appears in *Educational Administration Quarterly* titled "Responding to the Collective and Individual 'Best Interests of Students': Revisiting the Tension Between Administrative Practice and Ethical Imperatives in Special Education Leadership." He and contributor Peter Liesenfeld are good colleagues.

Cynthia Gerstl-Pepin is a Professor of Educational Leadership and Foundations at the University of Vermont. Her writing explores educational inequity, politics, and social justice leadership. Dr. Gerstl-Pepin served as a Fulbright Scholar at Beijing Normal University in the People's Republic of China. Based on her Fulbright scholarship, she coedited a book entitled *Survival of the Fittest: The Shifting Contours of Higher Education in China and the US.* She is also coauthor of the book *Reframing Educational Politics for Social Justice* and the coeditor of *Social Justice Leadership for a Global World* and *Reimagining the Public Intellectual in Education: Making Scholarship Matter.*

Marla Susman Israel is an Associate Professor in the School of Education at Loyola University, Chicago. She is the Graduate Program Director for the Department of Administration and Supervision. Her primary research and teaching areas are principal preparation, organizational change and school improvement, human resources, and ethics. She is the Assistant Director for Internet and Social Media for the New DEEL. Prior to joining Loyola, Dr. Israel was a building-level and district-level leader in Skokie, Waukegan, and Evanston, Illinois, serving English language learners and minority populations.

Lisa A.W. Kensler is an Associate Professor of Educational Leadership in the College of Education at Auburn University. Her original training as an ecologist continues to shape her research interests. Dr. Kensler's current research is focused on green schools and the leadership and learning required for transforming schools into more socially just, eco-logically healthy, and economically viable communities that engage intentionally with the global sustainability movement. She has published peer-reviewed articles and book chapters related to democratic commu-nity, trust, and whole-school sustainability.

Peter V. Liesenfeld attended Norman Public Schools, followed by the University of Oklahoma, earning a master's and a Ph.D. in Educa-tion Administration. He is currently Principal of Norman North High School. Peter's research has centered primarily on community engage-ment in the school setting, providing support and access to all students. In 2013, he presented findings involving community school develop-ment, including social and human capital development, at the UCEA Annual Values and Leadership Conference. Dr. Liesenfeld has devoted his career to giving back to the community that supported him through his childhood, and strives daily to make a difference in children's lives.

William J. Mathis is the Managing Director of the National Education Pol-icy Center at the University of Colorado, Boulder, and the former Super-intendent of Schools for the Rutland Northeast Supervisory Union in Brandon, Vermont. He was a National Superintendent of the Year final-ist and a Vermont Superintendent of the Year. He currently serves on the Vermont State Board of Education and chairs the legislative com-mittee. He has published or presented research on finance, assessment, accountability, standards, cost-effectiveness, education reform, history, and Constitutional issues. He also serves on various editorial boards and frequently publishes commentary on educational policy issues.

Rachel McNae is a Senior Lecturer of Educational Leadership and Pre-Service Teacher Education at the University of Waikato, Hamilton, New Zealand. Rachel's research agenda is founded on a firm belief for social justice and utilizes strength-based approaches to assist school lead-ers to enhance their leadership practices. Generating research that spans the fields of women and leadership, student voice, youth leadership, and leadership curriculum development in schools and communities, Rachel advocates for reshaping leadership learning in order to seek out and interrogate the relational aspects of leadership, so that these expe-riences are authentic, culturally responsive, relevant, and meaningful.

Michele Morrison is a Senior Lecturer in the Faculty of Education, Univer-sity of Waikato, New Zealand. Informed by her substantial practitioner experience, Michele's research and teaching focuses on educational leadership, coaching and mentoring, and initial teacher education. Her current research interests include the centrality of context in change leadership, school leadership for social justice, and school governance. The appointments of school principals by parent trustees, and tertiary pedagogies for leadership formation, feature in her recently published work.

Anthony H. Normore holds a Ph.D. from the University of Toronto. He is currently a Professor of Educational Leadership and Chair of Special Needs Services at California State University, Dominguez Hills. His research focuses on the preparation, growth, and development of urban school leaders in the context of ethics and social justice. Dr. Normore serves as the Book Series Editor of Advances in Educational Administration with Emerald Group Publishing.

Joseph A. Polizzi is an Associate Professor and Chair of the Education Department at Marywood University. He holds a Ph.D. in Educational Leadership from Pennsylvania State University. A former New York City public school English teacher, New York State Senate Fellow, and Fulbright Exchange Teacher, he currently directs an American Culture and English Language Summer Camp in Poland. His areas of research include authentic leadership, transformational learning, the use of films as a medium of instruction, and cross-cultural and international education. Dr. Polizzi lives in Clarks Summit, Pennsylvania with his wife, Eva, and daughters, Lily Julia and Sofie Joy.

Susan H. Shapiro is the Director of the Dillon Child Study Center at St. Joseph's College. She has served as a director of diverse preschools for over twenty years. Dr. Shapiro earned her bachelor's degree from Eugene Lang College, and a master's degree from Bank Street College of Education. She received her doctoral degree at New York University in Educational Leadership. Her dissertation examined the effects of 9/11/01 on early childhood directors. Dr. Shapiro has served as an instructor in higher education for online courses in educational leadership, has received grants for staff development in her schools, and has authored articles on ethical leadership.

Donnan Stoicovy is the Principal of Park Forest Elementary School in State College, Pennsylvania. Now in her twenty-sixth year, she has led her school's transformation into a learning laboratory for democracy, inquiry, community, and environment. Most recently, her school received the Emerald Award for Zero Waste efforts. She has developed partnerships with numerous community agencies and has created service learning projects, resulting in recognition of her school by the State of Pennsylvania as a "A School of Success." She carries a B.S. and M.Ed. in Elementary Education from Edinboro University of Pennsylvania, as well as a K–12

Administrative Certification. Currently, she is working on her doctorate in Curriculum and Supervision at the Pennsylvania State University.

Valerie A. Storey is an Associate Professor in the Department of Educational Leadership, School of Teaching, Learning and Leadership at the University of Central Florida, where she is the Director of the Ed.D. Executive Educational Leadership and the Ed.D. Education programs. She graduated with a Ph.D. in Educational Leadership and Policy Studies from Vanderbilt University, transitioning from over twenty years as a school administrator and instructional leader. Her research interest focuses on the preparation of educational leaders, emphasizing values and decision-making.

Jill Mattuck Tarule, Ed.D., is Professor Emerita, Educational Leadership and Policy, at the University of Vermont (UVM). She served as Associate Provost, Dean, other administrative roles, and as faculty in three institutions: Goddard College, Lesley College, and UVM. Her degrees are from Goddard College and Harvard Graduate School of Education, and an honorary doctorate from the University of New Hampshire School for Lifelong Learning. Coauthor of *Women's Ways of Knowing: the Development of Self* and *Voice and Mind,* and coeditor of *The Minority Voice in Educational Reform,* Dr. Tarule has published articles and chapters on women's leadership, adult learners, and leaders' moral decision-making.

Cynthia L. Uline is Professor Emeritus of Educational Leadership at San Diego State University (SDSU). Cynthia currently serves as Director of SDSU's National Center for the 21st Century Schoolhouse. Her research explores the influence of built learning environments on students' learning, as well as the role the public plays in shaping these learning spaces. Her research interests also include school leadership for learning, and school change and improvement. Cynthia's articles have appeared in journals such as *Educational Administration Quarterly, Teacher College Record, Journal of School Leadership, Journal of Educational Administration,* and *Journal of Research and Development in Education.*

Philip A. Woods is Professor of Educational Policy, Democracy and Leadership at the University of Hertfordshire, UK, Chair of the British Educational Leadership Management and Administration Society (BELMAS), and a Fellow of the Royal Society for the Arts. He is an internationally recognized scholar in the field of educational leadership and policy, with an extensive publication record focusing on issues such as democracy, educational policy and governance, distributed leadership, alternative education, and entrepreneurialism. His books include *Democratic Leadership in Education* (Sage, 2005), *Alternative Education for the 21st Century* (Palgrave, 2009, coedited with Dr. Glenys Woods), and *Transforming Education Policy: Shaping a Democratic Future* (Policy Press, 2011).

Index